SNIGLETS

RICH HALL & FRIENDS

Illustrated by Arnie Ten

MAGNOCARTIC *(mag no kar' tik)* n. Any automobile that, when left unattended, attracts shopping carts.

SNIGLETS

(*snig' lit*):
any word that doesn't appear in the dictionary, but should

Collier Books • Macmillan Publishing Company • New York

"Not Necessarily the News," a production of Not the Network Company, Inc., in association with Moffitt-Lee Productions, is produced by John Moffitt and co-produced by Pat Tourk Lee.

Macmillan Publishing Company
866 Third Avenue, New York, N.Y. 10022
Collier Macmillan Canada, Inc.

Library of Congress Cataloging in Publication Data

Hall, Rich, 1954-
Sniglets (snig' lit): any word that doesn't appear in the dictionary, but should.
1. Words, New—English—Anecdotes, facetiae, satire, etc. 2. Vocabulary—Anecdotes, facetiae, satire, etc.
I. Title.
PN6231.W64H3 1984 428.1'0207 84-1883
ISBN 0-02-012530-5

18 17 16 15

Designed by Antler & Baldwin, Inc.
PRINTED IN THE UNITED STATES OF AMERICA

For Pat Tourk Lee and Jessica Tourk

CONTRIBUTORS

Todd Adamson Randy S. Alton Masey Amara Michele Amendola Brian and Jennie Barber Mark Belden Dave Bertschy Seth Bishop Sarah and Tracy Blossom Rick Boehm Andrea Breare Anthony Brown Valerie Burrgart Nancy Burt George Cahlik Rob Caldwell Susan Cargen Chuck Carter Tracy Carter Bart Cassel Melissa Cazel David Chapman Kim Chicken Elissa Cohen B. Conover Patrick Coughlin Marshall Deacon Brian DeMoss Chuck DeVaughn Patricia Dowding Rachel Drury Bryan Duke D'Laine Dury Jill Dyer Nancy C. Edlund Mark Eisenburg Karen Elliot Ron Ferraro Dennis Frizie Sean Gallagher John Garazzi Chris Griffin **Rich Hall** Zoe Hall Stuart E. Hallett III Jimmy Halliday Wanda Harkins David Harrington Staci Haynes John L. Henderson III Scott Henderson Mike Herdon Michael L. Hofmann G. R. Howard Louis Hubbell James P. Humphrey Jim Inskeep Katrina Jameson Alice Johnson Damon Jones Rob Kamm Barbara Kansas Diana Kent Jeff Koob Lance Krystopher Kristin Kulak Teresa Lamke Jeff Lange Tammy Lauper Mary Lauzon Rick Lubben Rick Luttenberger R. A. MacDonald Edmund Marcantonio Jed Martinez Meredith Maslanka Randi McDonald Scott McDonald Andrea McFarland Yvonne McHale Jonathan McKee Tom Menchyk Billy and Kelly Merton Cheri Lynn Monahan Dave Moran Mike and Apryl Moran Kevin Morgan Betty Morlan Roger Nalevanko Pat Nash Dave Nolan M. Nuckols Annice O'Brien Karen O'Byrne Michaelin Otis John Palatano Eric R. Pfeffinger Kevin Phillips Gerry Picard Charles A. Pluta Melinda Pofahl Tom Poisseroux Rick Powell Randall Putala Rob Ramsey Lucinda Reph George E. Reynolds III Mary T. Ritenburg Schatzie Schaefers Jenny Schoen Andy Schumacher Lynne Schuman Mike Sharp Bob and Bonnie Simko Annie Singer Darrell E. Smith Paula D. Smith Tisha Smith Pam Soule Kathy Spear Russell Spiler, Jr. B. Starkweather Tawnya Steinbrecher John Stempa, Jr. Debbie Swiz Stephen Szczesuil Jerry Tapp Sean Templeton Trey Terry Anne Tessari Gerald Tidman Guy Torak Jessica Tourk Jim Tursi Jody Uchtmann Mike Upton Ashland Vaughn Joe Vigil Jr. Renee Werbonski Sean Watt Dee Webster Ramona M. Weeks Brenda Wegmann Matthew Weiss Kay Well Maridee Whitehead Byron S. Winchester, Jr. Brian Yetter and Vincent Hurley Randy L. York Jodi Zahler John M. Zelenak Julian Zelizer

CONTENTS

ABZOT
(ab' zaht)

n. The device in a currency changer that determines whether a bill is too wrinkled or not.

ACCORDIONATED
(ah kor' de on ay tid)

adj. Being able to drive and refold a road map at the same time.

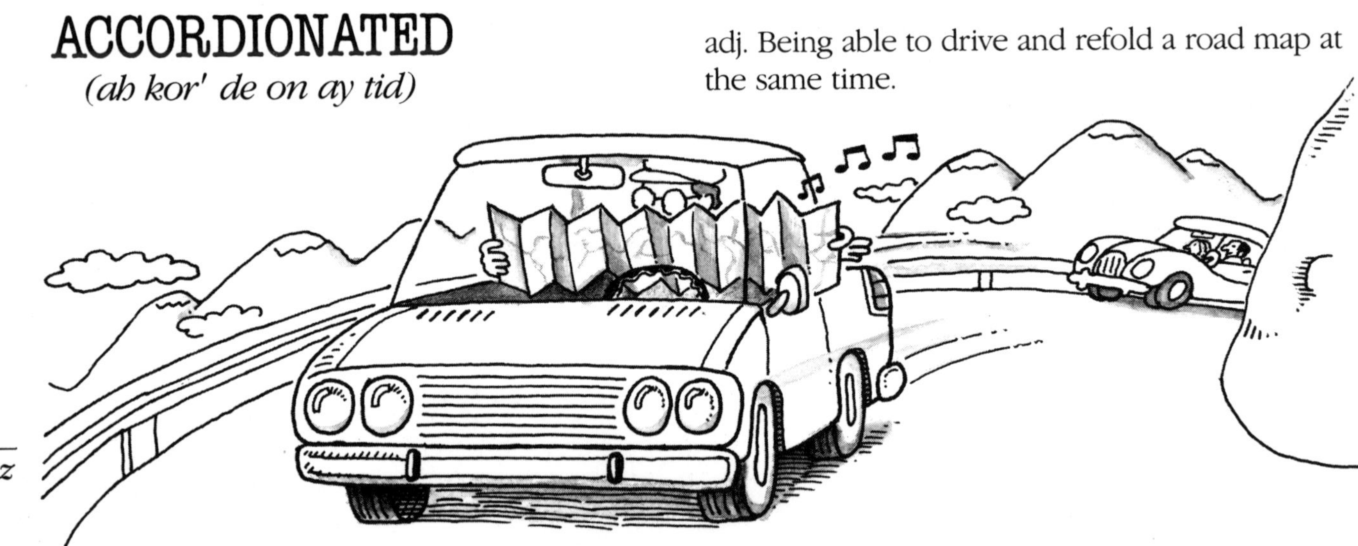

AEROMA
(ayr oh' ma)

n. The odor emanating from an exercise room after an aerobics workout.

AEROPALMICS
(ayr o palm' iks)

n. The study of wind resistance conducted by holding a cupped hand out the car window.

ALPONIUM
(al po' nee um)

n. (chemical symbol: Ap) Initial blast of odor upon opening a can of dog food.

AMBIPORTALOUS
(am bih port' ahl us)

adj. Possessing the uncanny knack for approaching a set of double doors and *always* pushing the locked one.

ANACEPTION
(an a sep' shun)

n. The body's ability to actually affect television reception by moving about the room.

ANTALIXIC
(ant a lik' sik)

n. One who passes over licorice jellybeans.

ANTICIPARCELLATE
(an ti si par' sel ate)

v. Waiting until the mailman is several houses down the street before picking up the mail, so as not to appear too anxious.

AQUADEXTROUS
(ak wa deks' trus)

adj. Possessing the ability to turn the bathtub faucet on and off with your toes.

AQUALIBRIUM
(ak wa lib' re um)

n. The point where the stream of drinking fountain water is at its perfect height, thus relieving the drinker from (a) having to suck the nozzle, or (b) squirting himself in the eye.

ARACHNIDIOT
(ar ak ni' di ot)

n. A person, who, having wandered into an "invisible" spider web begins gyrating and flailing about wildly.

ATTRINYL
(a try' nil)

n. (chemical symbol: At) A black, bulletproof, totally inflexible type of plastic, used primarily in covers of pay phone directories.

BANDILE

(ban' dyl)

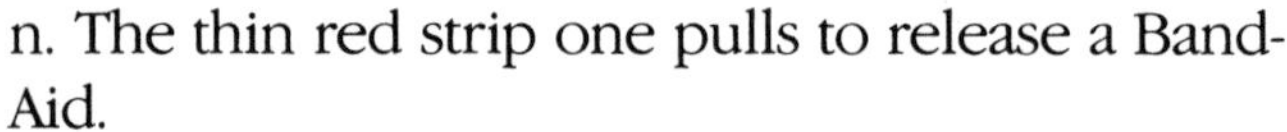

n. The thin red strip one pulls to release a Band-Aid.

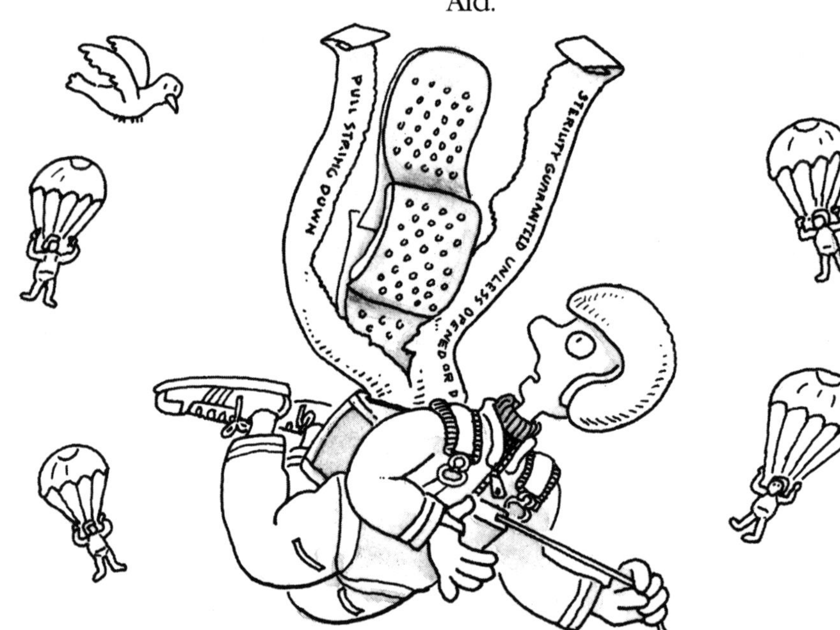

BARGARCS
(bar' jarks)

n. The streaks on a car's windshield from faulty wipers.

BATHQUAKE
(bath' kwake)

n. The violent quake that rattles the entire house when the water faucet is turned to a certain point.

BEVAMETER
(bev' a meet uhr)

n. (a unit of measure) The distance a coaster, attached to the bottom of a wet glass, will travel before it falls back to earth.

BLEEMUS
(blee' mus)

n. The disgusting film on the top of soups and cocoa that sit out for too long.

BLIBULA
(blih' byu luh)

n. The spot on a dog's stomach which, when rubbed, causes his leg to rotate wildly.

BLINDELIZE
(blin' dul eyes)

v. To scratch an album beyond recognition trying to maneuver it over the record spindle.

BLITHWAPPING
(blith' wap ing)

v. Using anything BUT a hammer to hammer a nail into the wall, such as shoes, lamp bases, doorstops, etc.

BLIVETT
(blih' vit)

v. To turn one's pillow over and over, looking for the cool spot.

BLOTCH
(blahch)

v. To slap the bottom of a catsup bottle with increasing intensity, ultimately resulting in BLOTCHSLIDE.

BOBBLOGESTURE
(bah blo jes' cher)

n. The classroom activity of not knowing an answer but raising one's hand anyway (after determining a sufficient number of other people have also raised their hands, thus reducing the likelihood of actually being called on).

BOSLUM
(bahz' lum)

n. The small metal ring on a ballpoint pen that separates the top half (MELANEXUS) from the bottom half (MOOSTERUS).

BOVILEXIA

(bo vil eks' e uh)

n. The uncontrollable urge to lean out the car window and yell "Moo!!" every time you pass a cow.

BRATTLED
(brat' uld)

adj. The unsettling feeling, at a stoplight, that the busload of kids that just pulled up beside you is making fun of you.

BRIMPLET
(brim' plit)

n. A frayed shoelace that must be moistened to pass through a shoe eyelet.

BUCKLINT
(buck' lint)

n. The fine red and blue threads running through new dollar bills.

BUCULETS
(buk' u lets)

n. The bumper guards on the underside of a toilet seat.

BUMPERGLINTS
(bump' ur glintz)

n. The small reflective obstacles in the middle of interstate highways which supposedly keep drivers awake and on the track.

BURBULATION
(ber byu lay' shun)

n. The obsessive act of opening and closing a refrigerator door in an attempt to catch it before the little automatic light comes on.

BURSPLOOT
(ber' sploot)

v. To position one's thumb at the end of a garden hose to increase the water pressure.

BUSBLENDER
(bus' blen dur)

n. The device at the front of the bus that tosses your fare around for awhile, then swallows it.

CABNICREEP
(kab' nih kreep)

n. The structural condition in which the closing of one kitchen cabinet causes another to open.

CAREENA
(ka reen' uh)

n. Any mangled or missing piece of highway guard rail.

CARPERPETUATION
(kar' pur pet u a shun)

n. The act, when vacuuming, of running over a string or a piece of lint at least a dozen times, reaching over and picking it up, examining it, then putting it back down to give the vacuum *one more chance*.

CEREOALLOCATIVE
(ser e o al'o ka tuv)

adj. Describes the ability of a seasoned breakfast eater to establish a perfect cereal/banana ratio, assuring there will be at least one slice of banana left for the final spoonful of cereal.

CHALKTRAUMA
(chawk' traw ma)

n. The body's reaction to someone running his fingernails down a chalkboard.

CHARP
(charp)

n. The green, mutant potato chip found in every bag.

CHEEDLE
(chee' dul)

n. The residue left on one's fingertips after consuming a bag of Cheetos.

CHOCONIVEROUS

(chahk o niv' ur us)

adj. The tendency when eating a chocolate Easter bunny to bite off the head first.

CHWADS
(chwadz)

n. The small, disgusting wads of chewed gum commonly found beneath table and counter tops.

CIGADENT
(sig' a dent)

n. Any accident involving a cigarette: for instance when it sticks to your lips while your fingers slide off and get burned.

CINEMUCK
(si' ne muk)

n. The combination of popcorn, soda, and melted chocolate which covers the floors of movie theaters.

CIRCLOCRYOGENIC THEORY
(sur klo kri o jen' ik the' uh ree)

n. Postulates that no matter which way you turn a glass of ice water, the cubes will move to the back. (Further research has established that one piece of ice will always stick to the bottom of an empty glass until tapped, at which point it will come forward and smack the drinker on the end of his nose.)

CIRCULOIN TECHNIQUE
(sur' kew loyn tek neek')

n. The popular approach to steak dining in which one eats around the edges first, then works his way toward the middle.

CLUMFERT
(klum' furt)

n. The invisible extra step at the top and bottom of a staircase. Usually materializes when one is carrying a large bag of groceries.

COEGGULANT
(ko eg' yu lent)

n. The white things in a plate of scrambled eggs.

CONAGRAPHS
(kohn' a grafs)

n. The raised relief squares on an ice cream cone.

CREEDLES
(kre' dulz)

n. The colony of microscopic indentations on a golf ball.

CRUMMOX
(krum' oks)

n. The cereal that gets caught between the inner lining and the side of the box. Also, the leftover amount at the bottom. (Not enough to eat, but too much to throw away.)

CURBSWELL

(kerb' swel)

n. A seismic condition in which the curb on the passenger side of a car will rise and wedge a car door. The passenger must then climb out and stand on the curb until the swelling goes down.

DASHO
(da' show)

n. The area between a car's windshield and dashboard, where coins, pencils, etc. cannot be humanly retrieved.

DETERRENCY
(de ter' ren see)

n. The ruined currency found in pants pockets after laundering.

DETRUNCUS
(de trunk' us)

n. The embarrassing phenomenon of losing one's bathing shorts while diving into a swimming pool.

DISCONFECT
(dis kon fekt')

v. To sterilize the piece of candy you dropped on the floor by blowing on it, somehow assuming this will "remove" all the germs.

DOOR SLINKY
(dor slin' kee)

n. The springy device attached to the back of a door that prevents the door from marring the wall.

DUBLECTATE
(duh blek' tayt)

v. To misplace one's eyeglasses and eventually discover them atop one's head.

ECNALUBMA
(ek na lub' ma)

n. A rescue vehicle which can only be seen in the rear-view mirror.

ELBONICS
(el bon' iks)

n. The actions of two people maneuvering for one armrest in a movie theater.

ELECELLERATION
(el a cel er ay' shun)

n. The mistaken notion that the more you press an elevator button the faster it will arrive.

EQUATT
(e' kwat)

n. The pastime of trying to balance the light switch in the exact middle of the wall plate, so that the light is half on, half off.

ERDU
(uhr' dew)

n. The leftover accumulation of rubber particles after erasing a mistake on a test paper.

ESCALASTICIZE
(esk a last' i size)

v. To lean against the rail of a moving escalator and have the sensation of being pulled in opposite directions.

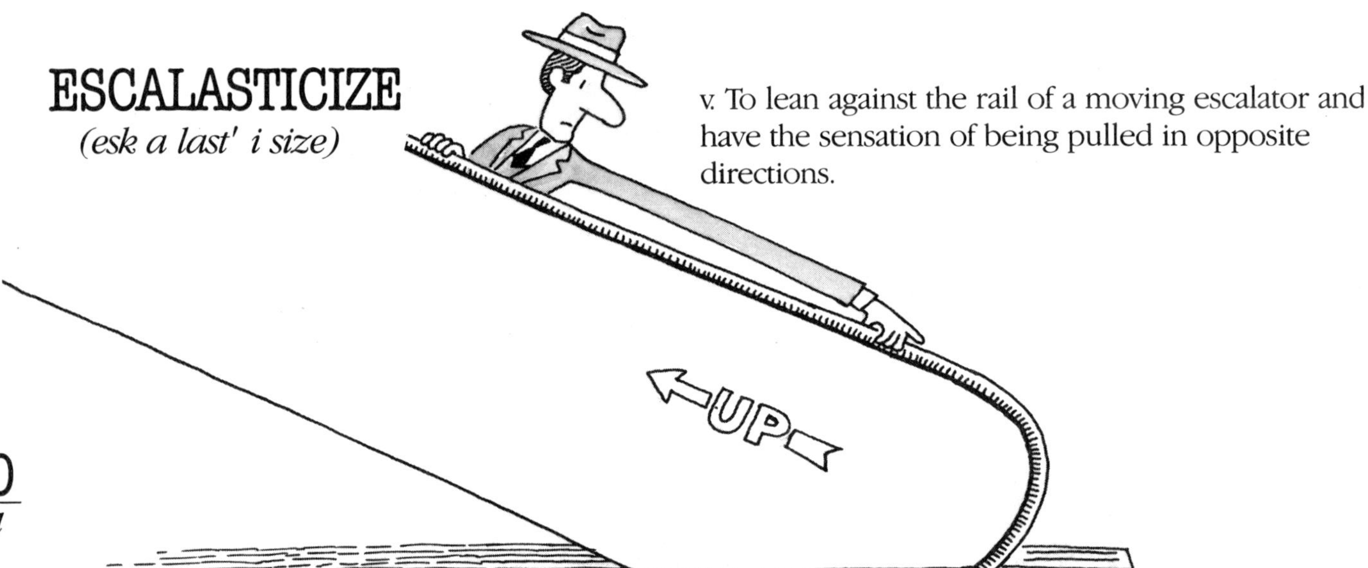

EUNEEBLIC
(you nee' blik)

n. A person who refuses to believe an "out of order" sign and risks his money anyway.

EXPRESSHOLES
(eks pres' holz)

n. People who try to sneak more than the "eight items or less" into the express checkout line.

FENDERBERG
(fen' dur burg)

n. The large glacial deposits that form on the insides of car fenders during snowstorms.

FLANNISTER
(flan' is tur)

n. The plastic yoke that holds a six-pack of beer together.

FLEN
(flen)

n. (chemical symbol: Fl) The black crusty residue that accumulates on the necks of old catsup bottles.

FLEPTIC
(flep' tik)

adj. The tendency of soup and dog food lids to slip into the can upon opening.

FLIRR
(flur)

n. A photograph that features the camera operator's finger in the corner.

FLOLES
(flolz)

n. The extra (fourth and fifth) holes in notebook paper. Created in the hopes that one day mankind will perfect a "five ring binder."

FLOPCORN
(flop' korn)

n. The unpopped kernels at the bottom of the cooker.

FLOTION
(flo' shun)

n. The tendency when sharing a waterbed to undulate for five minutes every time the other person moves.

FLOTTA FACTOR
(flah' ta fak' tur)

n. The proven scientific fact that at a self-service pump, the last ten cents take longer to reach the tank than the first twelve dollars' worth.

FLOWFRIGHT
(flo' frite)

n. The desperate attempt by a homeowner to "talk" his overflowing toilet into backing down.

FLUGGLING

(flug' ul ing)

v. The dangerous practice, in a darkened room, of using one's finger to guide the end of an electrical plug into a wall socket.

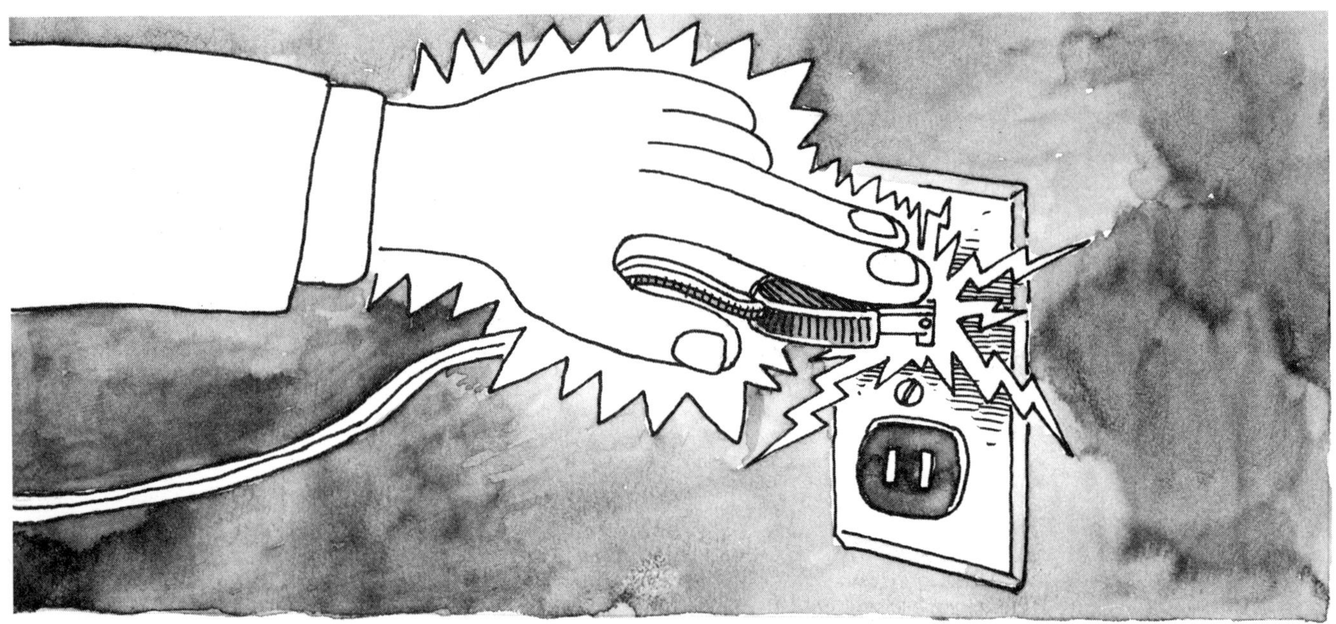

FRAZNIT

(frahs' nit)

n. Any string hanging from an article of clothing, which when pulled causes the article to completely unravel.

FRUST
(frust)

n. The small line of debris that refuses to be swept onto the dust pan and keeps backing a person across the room until he finally decides to give up and sweep it under the rug.

FURBLING
(fer' bling)

v. Having to wander through a maze of ropes at an airport or bank even when you are the only person in line.

FURNIDENTS
(fer' nih dents)

n. The indentations that appear in carpets after a piece of furniture has been removed.

FURTERUS ZONE
(fer ter' us zohn)

n. The empty stretches of bun on either end of a hot dog.

GARMITES
(gar' mitz)

n. Those items of clothing that fit perfectly in the store, but somehow shrink on the way home.

GENDERPLEX
(jen' dur pleks)

n. The predicament of a person in a theme restaurant who is unable to determine his or her designated bathroom (e.g., turtles and tortoises).

GERTATIOUS

(gur tay' shus)

adj. Having the adolescent fear that hanging one's arm over the bed at night will mean being dragged under.

GLACKETT

(glak' it)

n. The noisy ball inside a spray-paint can.

GLADHANDLING
(glad' han dling)

n. To attempt, with frustrating results, to find and separate the ends of a plastic-sandwich or trash bag.

GLANTICS
(glan' tiks)

n. Two people, who, while making out, open their eyes at the same time to see if the other is looking.

GLEEMULE
(glee' mule)

n. (a unit of measure) One unit of toothpaste, measured from bristle to bristle. (Not to be confused with GLEEMITES, which are petrified deposits of toothpaste found in sinks.)

GLUTETIC CHAIR
(glew tet' ik chair)

adj. A twentieth-century design of chair, found most often in movie theaters. The main feature of the Glutetic chair is its ability to keep folding up underneath a person as he tries to force it down with his rear.

GRACKLES
(grak' elz)

n. The wrinkles that appear on the body after staying in water too long.

GREELITE
(gree' lite)

n. The eerie glow that emanates from beneath escalator steps.

GRINION
(grin' yun)

n. The unsightly indentation in the middle of a belt when it has been worn too long.

GRIPTION
(grip' shun)

n. The sound of sneakers squeaking against the floor during basketball games.

GRISKNOB
(gris' nahb)

n. The end of a chicken drumstick which always gives the appearance of having more chicken on it.

GURMLISH
(gurm' lish)

n. The red warning flag at the top of a club sandwich toothpick which prevents the person from biting into it and puncturing the roof of his mouth.

HANGLE
(han' gul)

n. A cluster of coat hangers.

HEMPENNANT
(hem' pen ent)

n. Any coattail, cuff, or dress hem dangling outside the door of a moving vehicle.

HOZONE

(ho' zohn)

n. The place where one sock in every laundry load disappears to.

HUDNUT

(hud' nut)

n. The bolt left over when one has finished reassembling a bicycle or car engine.

HYDRALATION

(hi dra lay' shun)

n. Acclimating oneself to a cold swimming pool by bodily regions: toe-to-knee, knee-to-waist, waist-to-elbow, elbow-to-neck.

HYSTIOBLOGINATION
(his' te o blahg in ay' shun)

n. The act of trying to identify a gift by holding it to your ear and shaking it.

IDIOT BOX
(id' e ot bahks)

n. The part of the envelope that tells a person *where* to place the stamp when they can't quite figure it out for themselves.

IGNISECOND
(ig' ni sek und)

n. The overlapping moment of time when the hand is locking the car door even as the brain is saying "my keys are in there!"

JIFFYLUST
(ji' phee lust)

n. The inability to be the first person to carve into a brand-new beautiful jar of peanut butter.

KEDOPHOBIA

(ked oh fo' be uh)

n. The fear of having one's sneakers eaten by the teeth on the escalator.

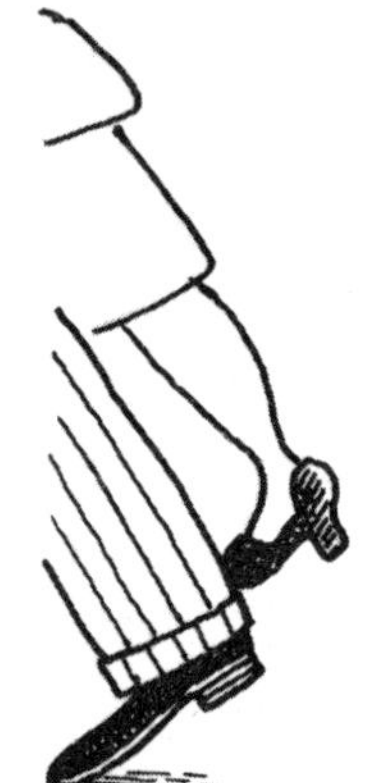

KNIMPEL
(nim' pul)

n. The missing last piece of a jigsaw puzzle.

KROGT
(krabt)

n. (chemical symbol: Kr) The metallic silver coating found on fast-food game cards.

LACTOMANGULATION
(lak' to man gyu lay' shun)

n. Manhandling the "open here" spout on a milk carton so badly that one has to resort to using the "illegal" side.

LAMINITES
(lam' in itz)

n. Those strange people who show up in the photo sections of brand-new wallets.

LOTSHOCK
(laht' shahk)

n. The act of parking your car, walking away, and then watching it roll past you.

LUB
(lub)

n. The small deposit of spinach that lodges itself between one's teeth.

McMONIA
(muk moan' ee uh)

n. (chemical symbol: Mc) Noxious gas created by fast-food employee mopping under your table while you're eating.

MAGGIT
(mag' it)

n. Any of the hundreds of subscription cards that fall from the pages of a magazine (pl. MAGGREGATE).

MAGNIPHOBIA
(mag ni fo' be uh)

n. The fear that the object in the side mirror is *much much* closer than it appears.

MANGLAZETTE
(mang la zet')

n. The newspaper at the top of the stack that everyone passes over, believing the ones beneath it have better or fresher news.

MARP
(marp)

n. The impossible-to-find beginning of a roll of cellophane tape.

MATTRESCOTTING
(mat' res kot ing)

n. The pattern of gray and white lines on an institutional mattress.

MAYPOP
(may' pahp)

n. A bald tire.

MEMNANTS
(mem' nents)

n. The chipped or broken *m&m's* at the bottom of the bag.

MERFERATOR
(mur' fur ay ter)

n. The cardboard core in a toilet tissue roll.

METHYLPHOBIA
(meth il fo' be uh)

n. The fear that you are going to have to pay for the one cent you over-pumped at the self-service station.

MITTSQUINTER
(mit' skwint ur)

n. A ballplayer who looks into his glove after missing the ball, as if, somehow, the cause of the error lies there.

MOPHENES

(mo' feenz)

n. The semi-truck headlights that invade your motel room at three in the morning.

MOTSPUR
(mot' sper)

n. The pesky fourth wheel on a shopping cart that refuses to cooperate with the other three.

MOWMUFFINS
(mo' muh finz)

n. The dried accumulation of grass on the underside of lawnmowers.

MUMPHREYS
(mum' freez)

n. (a useless sniglet) Those strange extra digits you find on push-button phones.

MUSQUIRT
(mus' kwirt)

n. The water that comes out of the initial squirts of a squeeze mustard bottle.

MUSTGO

(must' go)

n. Any item of food that has been sitting in the refrigerator so long it has become a science project.

NAPJERK

(nap' jurk)

n. The sudden convulsion of the body just as one is about to doze off.

NARCOLEPULACY
(nar ko lep' ul ah see)

n. The contagious action of yawning, causing everyone else in sight to also yawn.

NEGLINTICS
(ne glin' tiks)

n. The study of why dark lint attaches itself to light clothing and vice versa.

NEONPHANCY
(ne on' fan see)

n. A fluorescent light bulb struggling to come to life.

NERKLE
(nur' kel)

n. A person who leaves his Christmas lights up all year.

NEVITTS

(nev' itz)

n. The sandpaper-like deposits on a cat's tongue.

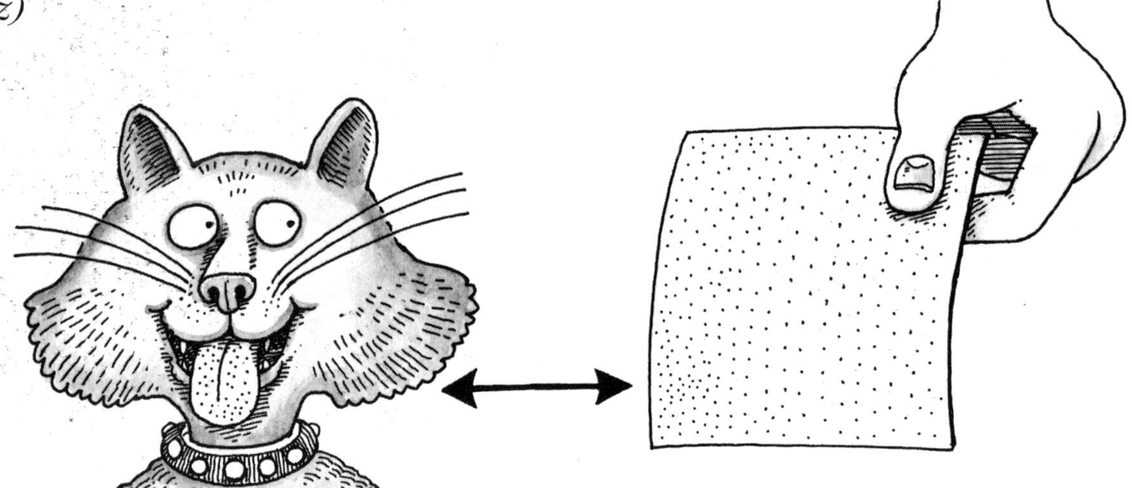

NISTOLS

(niz' tolz)

n. The small rubbery pads on the bottom of a dog's paw.

NIZ
(niz)

n. An annoying hair at the top of a movie screen.

OATGAP
(oht' gap)

n. The empty space in a cereal box created by "settling during shipment."

OPLING
(oh' pling)

n. The act, when feeding a baby, of opening and closing one's mouth, smacking one's lips and making "yummy" noises, in the hope that baby will do the same.

OPTORTIONIST
(op tor' shun ist)

n. The kid in school who can turn his eyelids inside out.

OROGAMI
(or oh ga' mee)

n. The miraculous folding process that allows Kleenexes to methodically emerge from the box one at a time.

OROSUCTUOUS
(or oh suk' chew us)

adj. Being able to hold a glass to one's face by sheer lung power.

PEDIDDEL
(pe did' ul)

n. A car with only one working headlight. (*Related to* LEDDIDEP: a car with only one working taillight.)

PEDLOCK
(ped' lahk)

n. The condition of a bicycle pedal wedging itself against the kickstand.

PELP
(pelp)

n. The crumbs and food particles that accumulate in the cracks of dining tables.

PENCIVENTILATION
(pen si ven ti lay' shun)

n. The act of blowing on the tip of a pencil after sharpening it.

PERCUBURP

(per' kyu berp)

n. The final gasp a coffee percolator makes to alert you it is ready.

PETRIBAR

(pet' ri bar)

n. Any sun-bleached prehistoric candy that has been sitting in the window of a vending machine too long.

PETROOL
(pet' rul)

n. The slow, seemingly endless strand of motor oil at the end of the can.

PEWTONE
(pyu tone')

n. (chemical symbol: Pu) A major atmospheric component of towns with paper mills.

PHISTEL
(fis' tul)

n. The brake pedal on the passenger side of the car that you wish existed when you're riding with a lunatic.

PHONESIA
(fo nee' zhuh)

n. The affliction of dialing a phone number and forgetting whom you were calling just as they answer.

PHOSFLINK
(fos' flink)

v. To flick a bulb on and off when it burns out (as if, somehow, that will bring it back to life).

PHOTOYOKEL

(fo to yo' kul)

n. A person who presses the wrong button on a film camera causing it to dismantle.

PHOZZLE
(fo' zul)

n. The buildup of dust on a record needle.

PICKLETTULANCE
(pik ul et' yu lans)

n. The ability to remember the entire family's order at a fast-food restaurant.

PIFFLESQUIT
(pif' ul skwit)

n. The wire net surrounding the cork of a champagne bottle.

PILLSBURGLAR
(pilz' berg ler)

n. Person able to sample the icing on a new cake without leaving a fingerprint.

PIYAN

(pi' an)

n. (acronym: "Plus If You Act Now") Any miscellaneous item thrown in on a late night television ad. (Example: a pitchman trying to sell an all purpose carving knife . . . "it's the only knife you'll ever need. Plus if you act now, this complete set of steak knives . . .")

POINT BLIMFARK

(poynt blim' fark)

n. The point at which the wheels on a stagecoach appear to turn in the opposite direction.

PORKUS NON GRATIS

(por' kus non grat' is)

n. The scraggly piece of bacon at the bottom of the package.

PREMBLEMEMBLEMATION

(prim blum em blum ay' shun)

n. Whenever you drop a letter in the mailbox, you always re-check to make sure it's gone down.

PROFANITYPE

(pro fan' i tipe)

n. The special symbols used by cartoonists to replace swear words (points, asterisks, stars, and so on). It is yet to be determined which specific character represents which specific expletive.

PSYCHOPHOBIA
(sy ko fo' be uh)

n. The compulsion, when using a host's bathroom, to peer behind the shower curtain and make sure no one is waiting for you.

PUPKUS
(pup' kus)

n. The moist residue left on a window after a dog presses its nose to it.

PURPITATION
(per pi tay' shun)

v. To take something off the grocery shelf, decide you don't want it, and then put it in another section.

RETROCARBONIC
(ret ro kar bon' ik)

n. Any drink machine that dispenses the soda before the cup.

RICEROACH
(rys' rohch)

n. The burnt krispie in every bowl of Rice Krispies.

RIGNITION
(rig ni' shun)

n. The embarrassing action of trying to start one's car with the engine already running.

ROCKTOSE
(rok' tohs)

n. The hard lumps that block the pouring spouts of sugar dispensers.

ROVALERT
(ro' val urt)

n. The system whereby one dog can quickly establish an entire neighborhood network of barking.

RUBUNCLES
(ru' bunk ulz)

n. The bumps on an uncooked chicken.

SARK
(sark)

n. The marks left on one's ankle after wearing tube socks all day.

SCADINK
(ska' dink)

n. The annoying buildup of ink on the end of a ball-point pen.

SCANDROIDS
(skan' droydz)

n. The striped price codes which mysteriously began appearing on consumer products a few years ago.

SCHLATTWHAPPER
(shlat' wap ur)

n. The window shade that allows itself to be pulled down, hesitates for a second, then snaps up in your face.

SCHNUFFEL
(shnuf' ul)

n. A dog's practice of continuously nuzzling your crotch in mixed company.

SCRIBLINE
(skrib' line)

n. The blank area on the back of credit cards where one's signature goes.

SCRIT
(skrit)

n. Anything that's been in the same place for at least fifty years without being used, such as the archaic bottles of hair tonic on a barber's counter.

SHIRTLOP
(shurt' lahp)

n. The condition of a shirt that has been improperly buttoned.

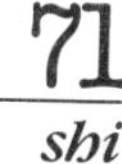

SHOEFLY
(shew' fliy)

n. The aeronautical terminology for a football player who misses the punt and launches his shoe instead.

SHUGGLEFTULATION
(shug lef tuyl ay' shun)

n. The actions of two people approaching, trying to get around each other, and muttering "thanks for the dance."

SIRLINES
(sir' lines)

n. The lines on a grilled steak.

SLACKJAM
(slak' jam)

n. The condition of being trapped in one's own trousers while trying to pull them on without first removing shoes.

SLOOPAGE

(slu' paj)

n. The tendency of hot dogs, hamburgers, and sandwich contents to slip from between their covers.

SLOTGREED
(slot' greed)

n. The habit of checking every coin return one passes for change.

SLURM
(slerm)

n. The slime that accumulates on the underside of a soap bar when it sits in the dish too long.

SLUTURES
(slew' chers)

n. The four white threads that protrude from Levis after the tag has been removed.

SNORFING
(snorf' ing)

n. The little game waitresses love to play of waiting until your mouth is full before sneaking up and asking, “Is everything okay?”

SPAGMUMPS
(spag' mumps)

n. Any of the millions of Styrofoam wads that accompany mail-order items. (*Also*, SPAGBULLIONS: custom fitted Styrofoam blocks that accompany stereo equipment.)

SPECLUMS
(spek' lums)

n. The miniscule bumps on a strawberry.

SPERAWS
(sper' awz)

n. The pinched marks on the ends of hot dogs.

SPIBBLE
(spib' ul)

n. The metal barrier on a rotary phone that prevents you from dialing past 0.

SPIROBITS
(spy' ro bits)

n. The frayed bits of left-behind paper in a spiral notebook.

SPIRTLE
(spur' tul)

n. The fine stream from a grapefruit that always lands right in your eye.

SPORK
(spork)

n. The combination spoon/fork you find in fast food restaurants.

SPRATCHETT
(spra' chit)

n. The rubber bar at a checkout counter that separates one load of groceries from another.

SPUBBLING
(spub' ling)

v. The superhuman feat of trying to wash one's hands and manipulate the "water saving" faucets at the same time.

SQUALKEENUS
(skwal ke' nus)

n. The shock syndrome that comes from biting into a popsicle with one's front teeth.

SQUATCHO
(skwatch' oh)

n. (another useless sniglet) The button at the top of a baseball cap.

STROODLE

(stru' dul)

n. The annoying strand of cheese stretching from a slice of hot pizza to one's mouth.

STRUMBLE
(strum' bul)

n. That invisible object you always pretend made you trip, when it was actually your own stupid clumsiness.

STURP
(sterp)

v. To pin down a runaway piece of paper or currency with one's foot before the wind blows it away.

SUBNOUGATE
(sub new' get)

v. To eat the bottom caramels in a candy box and carefully replace the top level, hoping no one will notice.

SUCCUBEEBISH
(suk yu be' bish)

n. The gelatinous substance found surrounding canned hams and Vienna sausages.

SUPERFLUHOLES

(sup ur flew' holz)

n. (another useless sniglet) The phony holes on speaker covers, put there to match the ones that actually surround the speaker.

TELECRASTINATION

(tel e kras tin ay' shun)

n. The act of always letting the phone ring at least twice before you pick it up, even when you're only six inches away.

TELEPRESSION

(tel e pre' shun)

n. The deep-seated guilt which stems from knowing that you did not try hard enough to "look up the number on your own" and instead put the burden on the directory assistant.

THERMALOPHOBIA
(thur muh lo fo' be uh)

n. The fear when showering that someone will sneak in, flush the toilet, and scald you to death.

THERNOT
(ther' nut)

n. The cardboard rod on a hanger that prevents creasing in pants.

THRICKLE
(thri' kel)

n. The itch in the back of the throat which can't be scratched without making disgusting barnyard-type noises.

TIEFRIGHT
(ty' fryt)

n. The fear that no matter which way you turn the twist-tie on a loaf of bread, it is the wrong direction.

TILE COMET
(tyl kom' it)

n. Any streamer of toilet paper attached to your heel as you emerge from a public restroom.

TIREQUILLS
(tyr' kwils)

n. The small rubbery protrusions on new tires.

TOASTATE
(tohs' tayt)

v. To impatiently pop toast up and down in the toaster, thus increasing the likelihood of burning it.

TOLLOAF
(toe' lohf)

v. Act of missing a toll basket and having to climb out of your car to retrieve the coin.

TRITZ
(trits)

n. The holes in saltine crackers.

TWINCH
(twinch)

n. The movement a dog makes with its head when it hears a high-pitched noise.

UFLUATION
(yu flu ay' shun)

n. The peculiar habit, when searching for a snack, of constantly returning to the refrigerator in hopes that something new will have materialized.

UHFAGE
(uff' aj)

n. The unit for determining a television's age, that is, the amount of time it takes for the picture to appear once the set has been turned on.

UPULS
(yu' puls)

n. The blank pages at the beginning and end of books, presumably placed there so you can rewrite the ending.

VULCANT
(vul' kant)

n. (chemical symbol: Vu) The stale air that emanates from a flat tire.

WARBLOID
(war' bloyd)

n. The tiny device in cassette players that eats tapes.

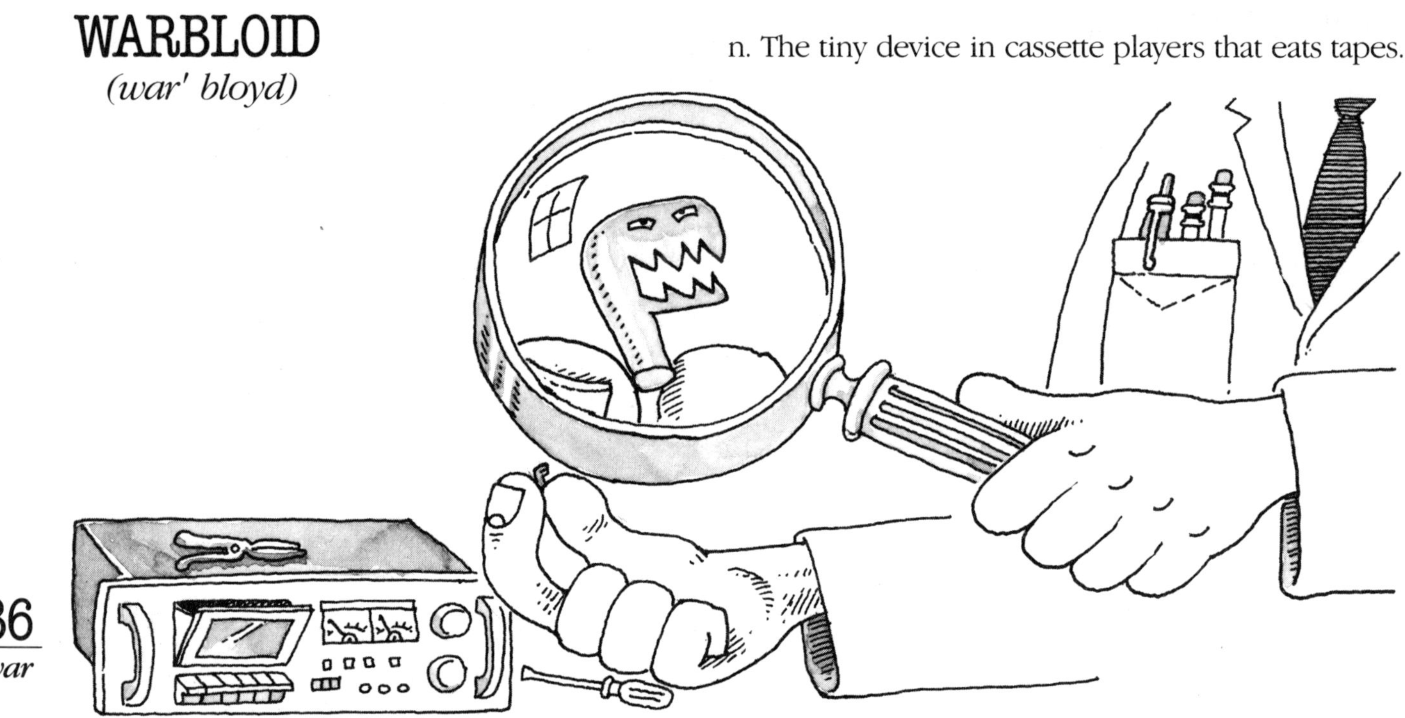

WATTBOBBLE
(wat' bah bul)

v. To remove a hot light bulb by turning it several seconds, letting your fingers cool, then repeating the process. This is generally followed by the glorious revelation of using your shirttail.

WERXILATION
(wurks ul ay' shun)

n. The property of some screen doors to start to slam shut only to catch themselves at the last moment and "float" to a gentle close.

WILY'S LAW
(wi' leez law)

n. The only known exception to Newton's Law of Gravity, Wily's Law states that an animal or person can suspend himself in midair provided (a) he is in a cartoon, and (b) he doesn't look down and realize he is no longer on solid ground.

WONDRACIDE

(wun' druh side)

n. The act of murdering a piece of bread with a knife and cold butter.

WURBLET
(wer' blit)

n. The line of moisture on one's trousers that comes from leaning against a wet counter in a public restroom.

n. Any word formed when typewriter keys jam together.

XIIDIGITATION
(ksi dij i tay' shun)

n. The practice of trying to determine the year a movie was made by deciphering the roman numerals at the end of the credits.

YARDRIBBONS
(yard rib' onz)

n. The unmowed patches of grass discovered after one has put away the mower.

YINKEL
(yin' kul)

n. A person who combs his hair over his bald spot, hoping no one will notice.

ZIBULA
(zi' bew luh)

n. The plastic spine which model car parts come attached to.

ZIMETER
(zi' me tur)

n. (a unit of measure) The last four or five inches of tape measure that never rewind automatically.

ZIPPLE
(zi' pul)

n. A broken poptop on a beer or soda can.

ZIZZEBOTS
(zi' ze botz)

n. The marks on the bridge of one's nose visible when glasses are removed.

ZYXNOID
(ziks' noyd)

n. Any word that a crossword puzzler makes up to complete the last blank, accompanied by the rationalization that there probably is an ancient god named Ubbbu, or German river named Wfor, and besides, who's going to check?

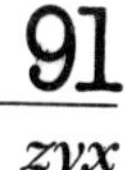

Appendix A

Anatomical Sniglets

CHINGRIP *(chin' grip)* n. Area where chin meets neck. Used for holding pillow when slipping on pillowcase.

GIMPLEXUS *(gim plek' sis)* n. Rear area of thighs, which must be peeled from car seat on hot summer days.

GLARPO *(glar' po)* n. The juncture of the ear and skull where pencils are stored.

GNARMBLUM *(narm' blum)* n. The dry wrinkly area at the end of the elbow.

GROMAXES *(grom' ack sis)* n. Inside area of knees used to grip steering wheel when holding a road map.

NUGLOO *(nug' lew)* n. Single continuous eyebrow that covers entire forehead.

SCRABITCH *(skrab' ich)* n. Impossible-to-reach area in middle of back which can never be scratched.

SNIFFLERIDGE *(snif' ul rij)* n. Trough leading from the nose to upper lip.

SWAZNA *(swaz' nuh)* n. The thin, disgusting membrane that connects the bottom of the tongue to the top of the jaw, presumably to hold it in place.

YINK *(yinc)* n. One strand of hair that covers bald spot.

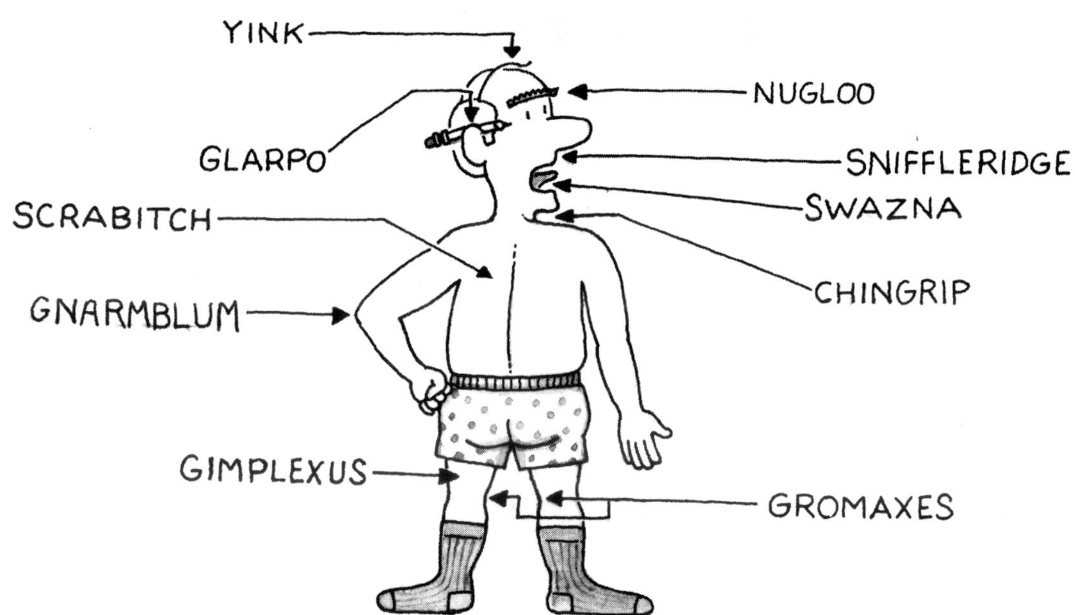
YINK
NUGLOO
GLARPO
SNIFFLERIDGE
SWAZNA
SCRABITCH
CHINGRIP
GNARMBLUM
GIMPLEXUS
GROMAXES

Appendix B

Extra Added Bonus Section for Poets

YORANGE
(yawr' anj)

n. Those disgusting white threads that hang from an orange after it has been peeled.

OFFICIAL SNIGLETS ENTRY BLANK

Dear Rich:

Here's my sniglet, which is every bit as clever as any in this dictionary:

____

____

____

____

____

Sincerely,

(name) ______________________________

(street address) ______________________________

(city, state, zip code) ______________________________

SNIGLETS
P.O. Box 2350
Hollywood, CA 90078

MORE SNIGLETS

RICH HALL & FRIENDS

Illustrated by Arnie Ten

ALPOPUCK *(al' po puk)* n. Any empty dish pushed around the kitchen floor by a dog trying to get the last morsel.

MORE SNIGLETS

(snig' lit):

any word that doesn't appear in the dictionary, but should

Collier Books • Macmillan Publishing Company • New York

"Not Necessarily the News," a production of Not the Network Company, Inc., in association with Moffitt-Lee Productions, is produced by John Moffitt and co-produced by Pat Tourk Lee.

Macmillan Publishing Company
866 Third Avenue, New York, N.Y. 10022
Collier Macmillan Canada, Inc.

Library of Congress Cataloging in Publication Data
Hall, Rich, 1954-
More sniglets.
1. Words, New—English—Anecdotes, facetiae, satire, etc. 2. Vocabulary—Anecdotes, facetiae, satire, etc.
I. Title.
PN6231.W64H33 1985 428.1'0207 84-29200

ISBN 0-02-012560-7
10 9 8 7 6

Designed by Antler & Baldwin, Inc.
PRINTED IN THE UNITED STATES OF AMERICA

*cover illustration:
MALIBUGALOO (*mal ih boo' guh lew*) n. A dance that affects barefoot beachgoers on hot summer days.

Hand lettering by Bernard Maisner

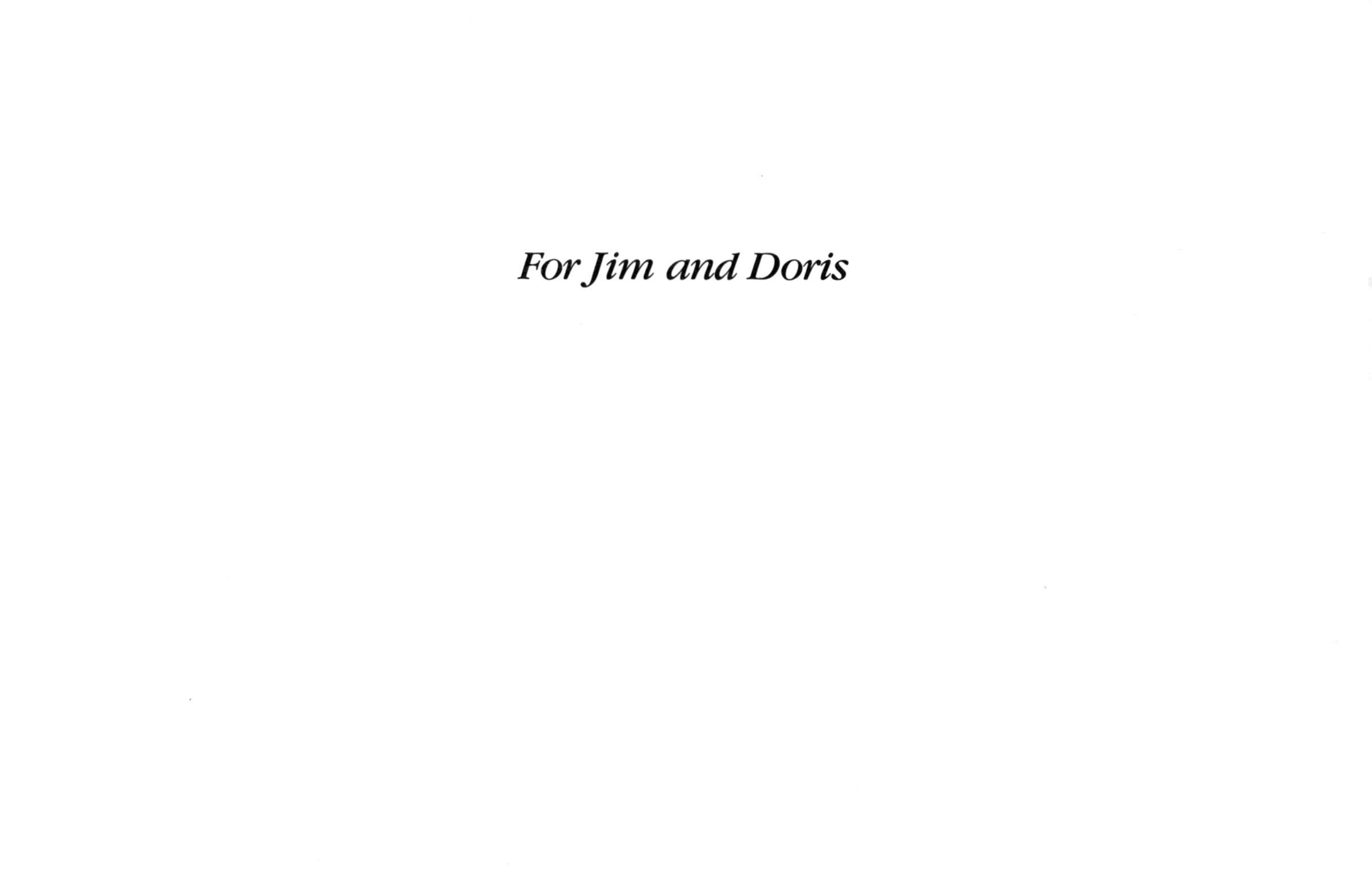

For Jim and Doris

CONTRIBUTORS

Jason Acquisto Keith Allen Frank Antonowitz Skip Balgemann Stephen Balsamo Richard Banford, Jr. Bobby Joe Barret Matt Besterman Jasper Borgman Greg Bowman Kim R. Brandt Judith Busman Mike Caldwell Dean Carignan Dave Carpenter Brian Clayton Irene Cole Thomas Cole Fred Conklin Elaine Coon Sandra Corigliano Stephen C. Coyle Leigh Cox Frances Curtis Andrea Dalzell Steve Danz Larry Davis David DeRouse Solange DeSantis Bruce Devino Ben Dickinson Steve Dings Margie Dodd Chris Dodson Terry Dugan Debbie Duplantis Brett Ellinsberg Melinda Ellis Pam Entzel Vince Fazzi Brian Fetcie Brian Fitzpatrick Tom Flynn Bill Forrester Tom Foy Bill Francis Bob Frederick Tom Gambaccini Richard Gan Caton Gates Chris Gaydash Ed Gilbert Dennis Gishwiller Steve Gitter Matt Glose Jay Green Kelly Haden **Rich Hall** Phillip Hamilton Michael J. Harris Will Hauptman David Hefferman Susan Helms Kenneth P. Henson Gail Hill Grant Howe Michael Hoyt Scott & Andie Janszen Malcolm & Ann Johnston Russ Josephson Scott Kafora Mike Karlovich Lawrence Kawcak Chris Keefe Ellen Keller Kate Watkins Klein Dan Koenig Bruce Kooken John Kozarich Barbara LaRochelle Dave Lurie Stacy Lynch Mark Majors Bill Mattia Bill May Allison McCarthey Randi McDonald Amanda Rae McNab Beth McShane John Miller Karma Miller Scott Milne Ray & Vikki Moggio Don Moore Nancy Moran Robert Mullins Brett Nagy Maryann Newby Neil Newman Bill Nilsson Mark Barker Nimick Carolyn Null Dan O'Conner Jeff Ogus Chris Ossanna Andy Parent Brent Parker Bruce Parker Mitch Pascal Gina Plude Sharon Potter Mike Rami Carl Reynolds Tony Russo Rick Samuels Michelle Anne Scantling John Schlosser Howard Schoeberlein Daniel Siciliano Tom & Laurie Skiro Emily & Jennifer Slatten Damian & Marian Smeragliualo Tana Sorenson Tom Spatig Louis Spurgeon Michael Stephany Tim Stewart Mike Stuper Roger Taylor Chris Terranova Rich Vanston Mark Vranges Brian Wargen Christa Warner Rona Weisberg E. Annette Wells Steve Wells Rob Whipple Greg Williams Reiko Williamson Rick Wilson Candy Woodyard

CONTENTS

AETS
(ehtz)

n. Greek symbols on water fountain handles.

AGONOSIS
(ag uh no' sis)

n. The syndrome of tuning into "Wide World of Sports" every Saturday just to watch the skier rack himself.

AIRDIRT
(ayr' dirt)

n. A hanging plant that's been ignored for three weeks or more.

ANCHORITY
(an chor' ih tee)

n. A group's final, hard-fought decision on what toppings to order on a pizza.

B+ STAMPEDE
(bee' plus stam peed)

n. The attempt by half the classroom to claim the paper with no name on it.

BACKSPACKLE
(bak' spak uhl)

n. Markings on the back of one's shirt from riding a fenderless bicycle.

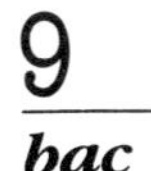

BACKSPUBBLE
(bak' spuh bul)

n. Dishwater that disappears down one drain of a double sink and comes up the other.

BALDAGE
(bald' aj)

n. The accumulation of hair in the drain after showering.

BANECTOMY
(bah nek' to mee)

n. The removal of bruises on a banana.

BARGUS
(bar' jus)

n. The area on the windshield that the wipers can't reach.

11
bar

BAZOOKACIDAL TENDENCIES

(bah zew' kuh sy dal ten' den seez)

n. The overwhelming desire of most individuals to reach out and pop the gigantic gum bubble billowing from someone's mouth.

BEAVO
(bee' vo)

n. A pencil with teeth marks all over it.

BIMP
(bimp)

n. A blurry or "double-edged" felt-tip marker.

BIXPLEX
(biks' pleks)

n. Psychological block in which a person cannot choose which color of disposable lighter to purchase.

BIZOOS
(bih zews')

n. The millions of tiny individual bumps that make up a basketball.

BLOOAGE
(blew' ij)

n. The residue left on fingers after using an S.O.S. pad.

BLURFLE
(bler' ful)

v. To be caught talking at the top of one's lungs when the music at the bar or disco suddenly stops.

BOMCA
(bahm' ka)

n. A lubricant derived from the salivary gland used for turning book pages.

BOWLIKINETICS
(boh lih kih neh' tiks)

n. The act of trying to control a released bowling ball by twisting one's body in the direction one wants it to go.

BRAZEL
(brah' zul)

n. The scratch plate on a matchbook.

BUBBLIC
(buh' blik)

adj. Addicted to the systematic popping of the bubbles in packing material.

BUGPEDAL
(bug' ped uhl)

v. To accelerate or decelerate rapidly in an attempt to remove a clinging insect from a car's windshield.

BURGACIDE

(burg' uh side)

n. When a hamburger can't take any more torture and hurls itself through the grill into the coals.

BUTTHENGE
(but' henj)

n. A pile of cigarette butts occupying a parking lot space.

BUTTNICK
(but' nik)

n. The crevice on an ashtray where the cigarette rests.

BUZZACKS
(buz' aks)

n. People in phone marts who walk around picking up display phones and listening for dial tones even when they know the phones are not connected.

CAFFIDGET
(ka fij' it)

v. To break up a Styrofoam coffee cup into several hundred pieces after consuming its contents.

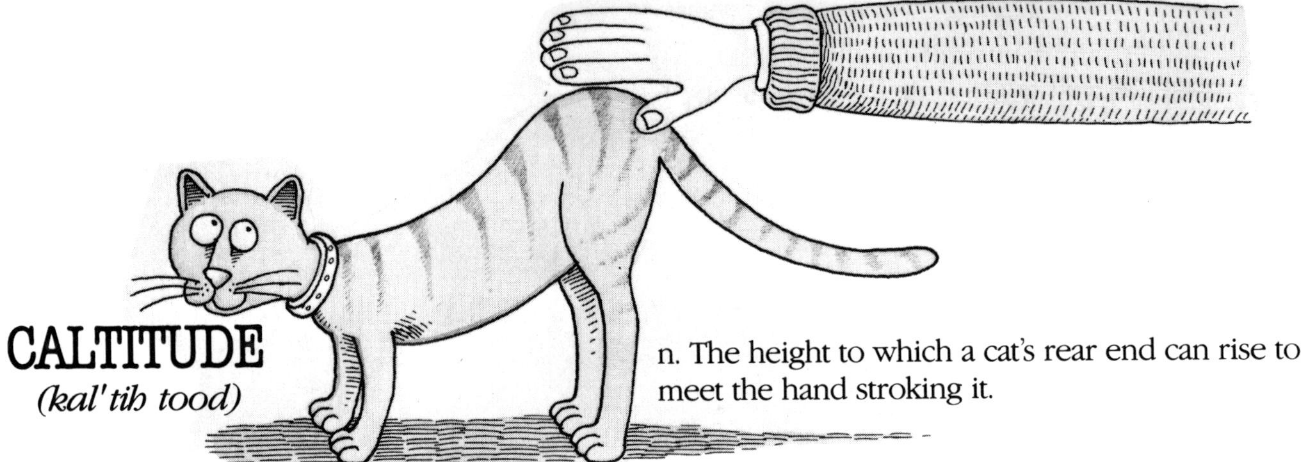

CALTITUDE
(kal' tih tood)

n. The height to which a cat's rear end can rise to meet the hand stroking it.

CARPERIMETER
(kar pur ihm' ih tur)

n. The zone between the wall and the end of the vacuum cleaner where dirt is "safe."

CATLAPSE
(kat' laps)

n. The amount of time a cat sleeping on his owner's lap has to awake and prepare to hit the floor before the owner stands up.

CELLOSTATIC
(sel oh stat' ik)

adj. The electrical property of cracker and cigarette wrappers that causes them to stick to your hand.

CHAIN GANG WALK
(chayn gang wok)

n. Activity observed in the footwear section of cheap department stores where the shoes are wired together "for your convenience."

CHECKUARY

(chek' yew air ee)

n. The thirteenth month of the year. Begins New Year's Day and ends when a person stops absent-mindedly writing the old year on his checks.

CHEERIOMAGNETIZATION

(cheer ee oh mag net i zay' shun)

n. The tendency of the last four or five Cheerios in the bowl to cling together for survival.

CHICLEXODUS
(chik ul eks' oh dus)

n. Any attempt by a gum ball to sneak out of the chute and roll past the buyer.

CHIPFAULT
(chip' fawlt)

n. The stress point on a potato chip where it breaks off and stays behind in the dip.

CHUBBLE
(chuh' bul)

n. The aerobic movement combining deep-knee bends and sideward hops used when trying to fit into panty hose.

CIRCUMPOPULATE
(sur kum pop' yew layt)

v. To finish off a popsicle "laterally" because the "frontal" approach causes one to gag.

COMBILOOPS
(kom' bih lewps)

n. The two or three unsuccessful passes before finally opening a combination locker.

CORNICLE
(kor' nih kul)

n. Breaded "washer" left on the stick after eating a corndog.

COUNTERSAURUS
(kown tur sawr' us)

n. Any person who orders two pieces of cheesecake and a Tab.

THE CRANIAL STOMP
(the kray' nee uhl stomp)

n. A somewhat primitive dance performed by youngsters trying to step on the heads of their shadows.

CRAYOLLIA
(kray oh' lee uh)

n. The area on the refrigerator where kindergarten drawings are displayed.

CRINKS
(krinks)

n. Crevices and junctions where car wax gets in but doesn't get out.

CRUMBPLUMB
(krum' plum)

v. To attack a cereal box in an attempt to retrieve the prize.

CUBELO
(kyew' beh lo)

n. The one cube left by the person too lazy to refill the ice tray.

CUSHUP
(kush' up)

v. To sit down on a couch somehow causing the cushion next to you to rise.

DARF
(darf)

n. The least attractive side of a Christmas tree that ends up facing the wall.

DIGITRITUS
(dij ih tree' tus)

n. Deposits found between the links of a watchband.

DILLRELICT
(dil rel' ikt)

n. The last pickle in the jar that avoids all attempts to be captured.

DIMP
(dimp)

n. A person who insults you in a cheap department store by asking "do you work here?"

DIPWAVERS
(dip' way vurz)

n. People who raise their hands when riding on roller coasters.

DOGNUT
(dawg' nut)

n. The giant nut on the side of a fire hydrant.

DOORK
(dawrk)

n. A person who always pushes on a door marked "pull" or vice versa.

DOWNPAUSE
(down' pawz)

n. The split second of dry weather experienced when driving under an overpass during a storm.

DROOT
(drewt)

n. A Dorito with an unnatural fold in it.

DRYLOWGRAPHS
(dry' loh grafs)

n. Strange, unintelligible symbols that accompany the washing instructions on clothing labels.

EASTROTURF
(ee' stroh terf)

n. The artificial grass in Easter baskets.

EIFFELITES
(eye' ful eyetz)

n. Gangly people sitting in front of you at the movies who, no matter what direction you lean in, follow suit.

ELEVERTIGO
(el uh vur' tig oh)

n. The sensation one experiences when an elevator stops or takes off too suddenly.

ELMERDERMIS
(el mur durm' is)

n. The white sheath that surrounds the nozzle of a glue dispenser.

ESCALOS
(es' kah lohz)

n. People who always end up taking the long way around from escalator to escalator when moving from floor to floor in shopping malls.

EUFIRSTICS
(yew fur' stiks)

n. Two people waiting on the phone for the other to hang up first.

EXASPIRIN
(eks as' prin)

n. Any bottle of pain reliever with an impossible-to-remove cotton wad at the top.

EXECUGLIDE
(eks ek' yew glyd)

v. To propel oneself about an office without getting up from the chair. 31

exe

FERROLES
(fer' olz)

n. The holes in the bottom of a steam iron.

FETCHPLEX
(fech' pleks)

n. State of momentary confusion in a dog whose owner has faked throwing the ball and palmed it behind his back.

FICTATE
(fik' tayt)

v. To inform a television or screen character of impending danger under the assumption they can hear you.

FINNAGE
(fin' aj)

n. The act of watching your money swallowed up as your groceries ride the conveyor belt at the supermarket.

FLARPSWITCH
(flarp' swich)

n. The one light switch in every house with no function whatsoever.

FLIMPS
(flimps)

n. People (usually observed in waiting rooms) who have advanced the Evelyn Wood technique to the point where they can flip through a magazine without ever looking down from the clock.

FLINTSTEP
(flint' step)

v. To wind up one's feet before running away in fear. Common among cartoon characters.

FLURRANT
(flubr' ubnt)

n. The one leaf that always clings to the end of the rake.

FAMAMAGE
(fa mam' aj)

v. To eliminate any annoying engine noise by simply turning up the volume of the radio.

FODS
(fahdz)

n. Couples at amusement parks who wear identical T-shirts, presumably to keep from getting lost.

FOYS
(foyz)

n. Missing pieces of a jigsaw puzzle that you later find stuck to the underside of your arm.

FRANKFLUID
(frank flew' id)

n. The liquid at the bottom of hot dog packages.

FRUSTRA
(frus' trah)

n. The special plastic used in the manufacture of fast-food ketchup packets.

FUFFLE
(fuh' ful)

v. To assume, when dining out, that you are making things easier on the waitress by using the phrase "when you get a chance . . .".

FURBULA
(fer' byew luh)

n. The designated chewing area on a dog's back.

GANGLOOT
(gan' glewt)

n. Person who leaves all his ski passes on his jacket just to impress people.

GAPIANA
(ga pee ah' nah)

n. The unclaimed strip of land between the "you are now leaving" and "welcome to" signs when crossing state lines.

GAZINTA (÷)
(gah zin' tuh)

n. Mathematical symbol for division; also the sound uttered when dividing out loud. (Example: "Four *gazinta* eight twice.")

GIBBLE
(jib' buhl)

n. The sliding keyhole cover on a car trunk.

GIZZLEDIPPLERS
(gih' zul dip lurz)

n. Those annoying waving hands seen on the backs of Winnebagos (placed there by people too lazy to be friendly on their own).

GLAMP
(glamp)

n. The telescopic device used to retrieve golf balls from ponds.

GLUTE
(glewt)

v. To shake a sugar packet vigorously so as to move the contents to the bottom before tearing open.

GRANTNAP
(grant' nap)

n. The extra five minutes of sleep you allow yourself that somehow makes all the difference in the world.

GREEDLING
(gree' dling)

v. Pretending to read the inscription on the birthday card when you really just want to know how much the check is for.

GRINTIGER
(grin' tuh jer)

n. The numbered code on the back of a greeting card that, when deciphered, reveals the price.

GUMMERATOR
(gum' uhr ay ter)

n. The pointed rubber object on the end of some toothbrushes.

GYROPED
(jy' roh ped)

n. A kid who cannot resist spinning around on a diner stool.

HACULA
(hak' yew luh)

n. The last few inches of tape measure or lawn mower cord that refuses to rewind automatically.

HALVENT

(hav' ent)

n. A style of auto window, found in later models, that only rolls down halfway.

HOUNDWOUNDING

(hownd' wown ding)

n. Canine act of circling a spot three or four times before settling on it.

HUDNUT
(hud' nuht)

n. The leftover bolt or screw in any "some assembly required" project.

ICISION
(ih sih' zhun)

n. Delicate operation performed on Neapolitan-flavored ice cream in which one entire flavor is precisely and systematically removed. (See **KNUCK**.)

INKSLICK
(ink' slik)

n. A greasy spot on a piece of stationery or test paper.

IRANT
(eye' rant)

n. A seamless pistachio nut; a pistachio nut afraid to come out in public.

42

jav

JAVA-VU
(jah' vah-voo)

n. Phenomenon of constantly adjusting the sugar/ cream level of your coffee to your liking, only to have a waitress come along and ruin it again.

JOES OF ARC
(johz' uhv ark)

n. Tiny drops of Mr. Coffee that die on the burner after the pot is removed.

JUKEJITTERS
(jook' jit erz)

n. Fear that everyone thinks you picked the awful tune emanating from the jukebox when it was actually the person before you.

KAWASHOCK
(kah wah shahk')

n. Pulling into the last remaining parking spot only to discover a motorcycle there.

KEYFRUIT
(kee' froot)

n. The one apple, pear, or tomato in the stand that, when removed, causes all the others to tumble forward.

KNUCK
(nuk)

n. Ice cream collected on the back of the hand when scraping the last portions from the box.

KROGLING
(kroh' gling)

n. The nibbling of small items of fruit and produce at the supermarket, which the customer considers "free sampling" and the owner considers "shoplifting."

45

kro

LIMALOPE
(ly' muh lohp)

n. The disgusting foreskin on a lima bean.

LINENEE
(lih nen ee')

n. The member of a two-person folding team at the Laundromat who takes the sheet and completes the fold.

LODGECOMBING
(loj' coh ming)

n. Final reconnaissance before vacating a motel room.

LOGGIUM
(log' yum)

n. Water that drips from one's nose hours after swimming.

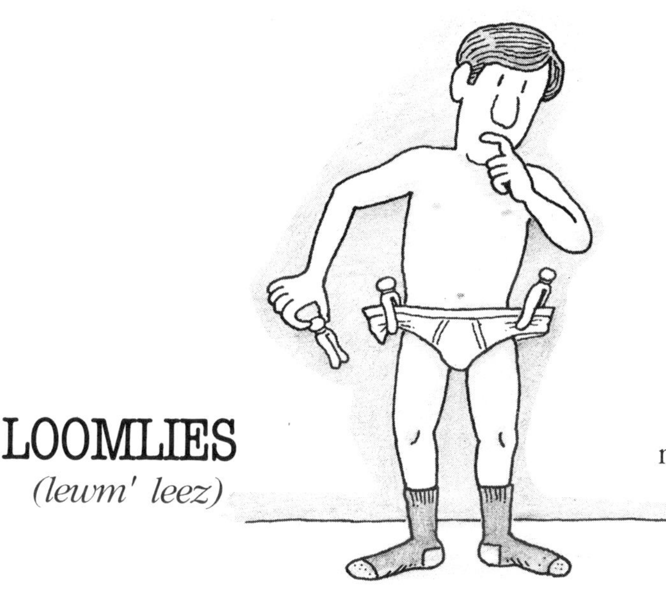

LOOMLIES
(lewm' leez)

n. Jockey shorts that have lost their elasticity.

LORP
(lawrp)

n. The part of the shoe that collapses when you try to pull it on without a shoehorn.

48

mag

MAGNAGRAM

(mag'nuh gram)

n. Any sign that takes on a new meaning when a magnetic letter falls off.

MALIBUGALOO
(mal ih boo' guh lew)

n. A dance that affects barefoot beachgoers on hot summer days.

MALTIAN
(mal' shun)

n. The alien beside you with concave cheeks, bulging forehead veins, and clearly outlined skull who is sucking on a too thick milk shake.

MANILLIUM
(mah nil' ee yum)

n. The lifespan of the clasp on a manila envelope before it breaks off and dies.

MICROTREK

(my' kro trek)

n. Any nervous trip to the microwave oven to make sure the food hasn't incinerated.

MICROTS

(my' krotz)

n. The two thumbnail-sized pieces you end up with when trying to remove a paper towel in a public washroom.

MIMOIDS
(mim' oydz)

n. People addicted to the smell of newly mimeographed test papers.

MISCORDANCE
(mis kawr' dans)

n. The principle that states: when reaching for drape cords, you will always tug on the wrong one first, practically tearing down the whole contraption.

MOPEEPS
(moh' peeps)

n. People compelled to look through the curtain opening of your motel room as they pass by.

MOTMESHS
(maht' mesh ez)

n. A pair of inseparable shopping carts.

MOTODRIFT
(moh' toh drift)

n. The mistaken belief at a stoplight that your car is moving backward when, actually, the car beside you is moving forward.

MOZZALASTICS
(maht suh las' tiks)

n. Large deposits of cheese that stick to the top of the pizza box.

MULTIPOCHOHOLES
(mul ti po' cho holz)

n. Wounds left in test papers from overerasing.

MUMMABOLIC CHORUS
(mum uh bah' lik ko' rus)

n. When three or more people are singing along to a tune and suddenly discover they are all faking their way through the unintelligible lyrics.

MUMMELOT

(muh' muh laht)

n. The bottomless repository where theatre tickets are dropped.

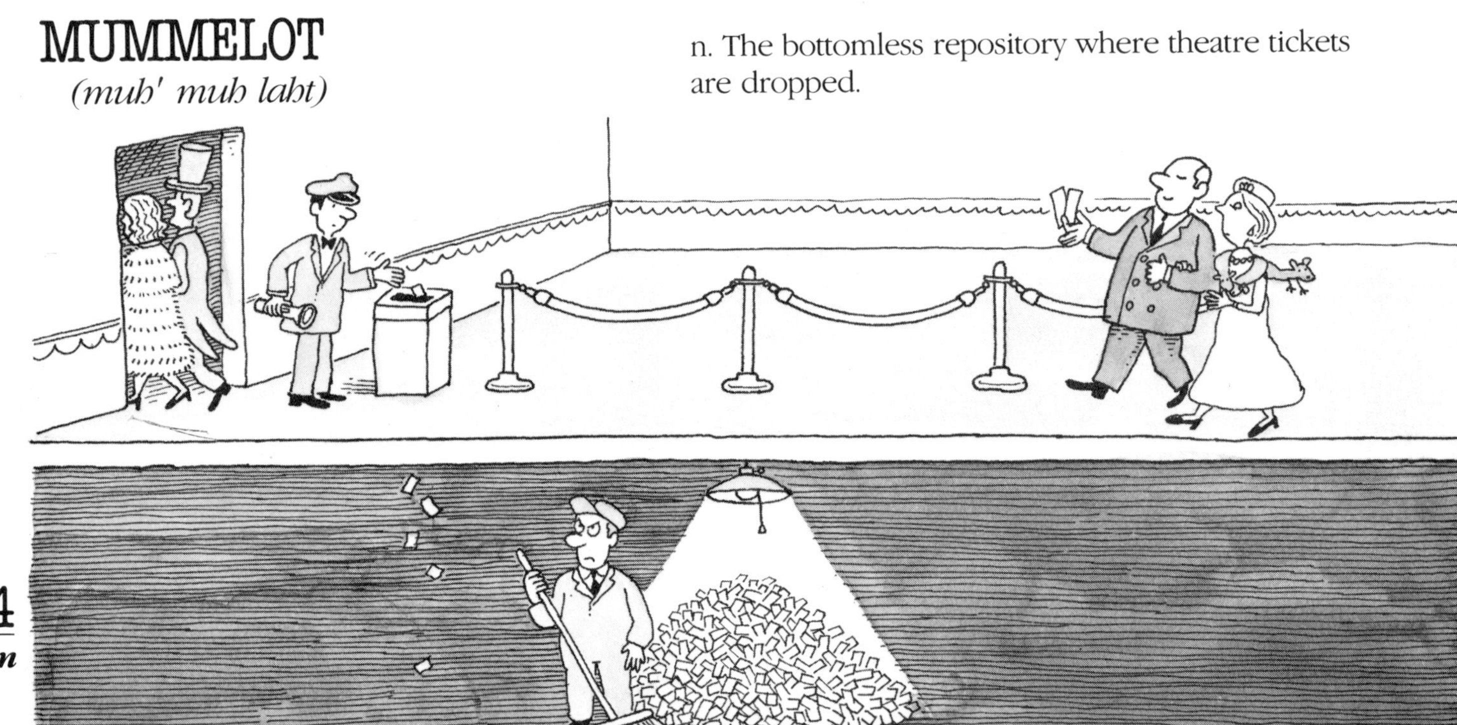

NEGATILE
(neh' guh tyl)

n. An area of the bathroom floor where, somehow, the scale registers you five pounds lighter.

NEOICE
(nee oh ice')

n. Any ice cube removed before its time that, upon close examination, resembles a carpenter's level.

NEUTRON PEAS
(new' tron peez)

n. Tiny green objects in TV dinners that remain frozen even when the rest of the food has been microwaved beyond recognition.

NEWTON
(new' tin)

n. The cookie shell surrounding the fig in a Fig Newton.

NICOMETEOR

(nik oh mee' tee awr)

n. A cigarette that exits through a car's front window and reenters through the back.

NIFLECK
(nih' flek)

n. The unmarked domino in the set.

NIZZLEBRILL
(nih' zuhl bril)

n. The "night-day" switch on a rearview mirror.

NOCTURNUGGETS
(nok' ter nuh gitz)

n. Deposits found in one's eye upon awakening in the morning, also called: GOZZAGAREENA, OPTIGOOK, EYEHOCKEY, etc.

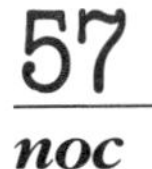

NOFLET
(nahf' lit)

n. The upward swirl of hair found on certain individuals such as Ronald Reagan and Big Boy.

NURGE
(nerj)

v. To inch closer to a stoplight thinking that will cause it to change quicker.

110 AT THE EQUATOR

(won' ten at the ek way' tawr)

n. Any burning sensation experienced directly below the navel when putting on a pair of jeans straight from the dryer.

OOPZAMA

(ewp' za muh)

n. Sudden scratching of scalp or face upon realization that the person you were waving at isn't who you thought it was.

OPUP

(op' uhp)

v. To push one's glasses back on the nose.

OREOSIS

(awr ee oh' sis)

n. The practice of eating the cream center of an Oreo before eating the cookie outsides.

OTISOSIS

(oh tis oh' sis)

n. The inability to meet anyone else's eyes in an elevator.

PAJANGLE
(pah jan' gul)

n. Condition of waking up with your pajamas turned 180 degrees.

P.A.T. (PERCUSSIVE ACCORDION-TROMBONE) METHOD

(pee ay tee meth' uhd)

n. Standard approach to preparing a straw for use. Consists of driving it sharply downward against a table top, thus causing the wrapper to rip open and achieve an "accordion" effect. The user then brings the exposed end of the straw to his mouth and blows the wrapper across the room.

PEDAERATION

(ped air ay' shun)

n. Perfect body heat achieved by having one leg under the sheet and one hanging off the edge of the bed.

PEPPIÉR

(pehp ee ay')

n. The waiter at a fancy restaurant whose sole purpose seems to be walking around asking diners if they want ground pepper.

PERCAMBULATE
(pur kam' byew layt)

v. Tendency of fitted sheets to lose their grip and roll up the mattress.

PERMAPRESSION
(pur' muh preh shun)

n. The discovery that there is no real difference in the various cycles of your washing machine.

PETONIC
(peh ton' ik)

adj. One who is embarrassed to undress in front of a household pet.

PHILOPOLOGIST
(fil ah pahl' ah jist)

n. A specialist who loads people onto amusement rides.

PIELIBRIUM
(py lih' bree uhm)

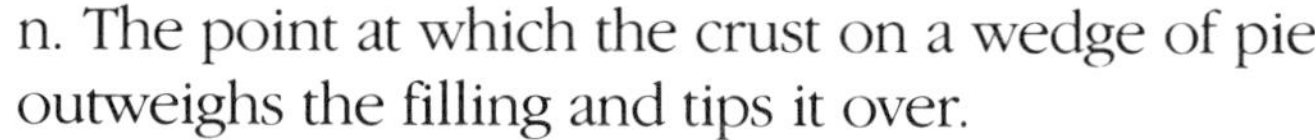

n. The point at which the crust on a wedge of pie outweighs the filling and tips it over.

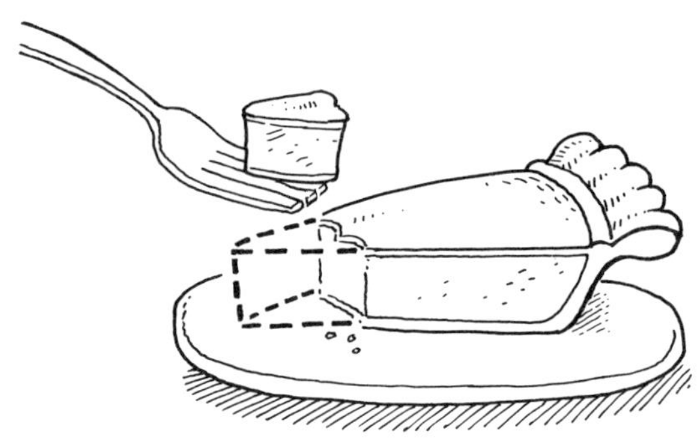

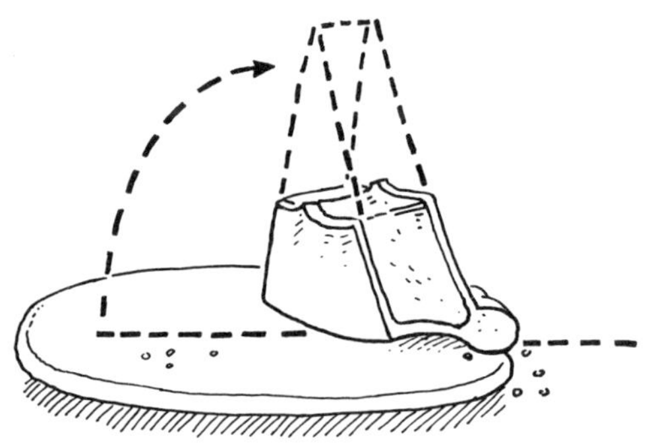

PIEPUSHERS
(py' puh shurz)

n. Attendants at fast food restaurants who, no matter what you order, try to unload apple or cherry turnovers on you.

PIEWAGON

(py' wa gun)

n. The small vehicle that carries game pieces around a Trivial Pursuit board.

PIGSLICE

(pig' slys)

n. The last unclaimed piece of pizza that everyone is secretly dying for.

POCKALANCHE
(pok' uh lansh)

n. Perpetual action of reaching down to pick up an item fallen from a shirt pocket, only to have another item fall out.

POLARIND
(poh' luh rynd)

n. The peeling on a Polaroid snapshot.

PORCELATOR
(pawr' suh lay tawr)

n. The hole near the rim of a bathroom sink.

POSICRO
(pah' sih kro)

n. The magnetic or "charged" strip of Velcro. *ant* NEUCRO (new' kro) n. The negative or "uncharged" strip of Velcro that *Posicro* adheres to.

POSTALPORTS
(poh' stuhl pawrtz)

n. The annoying windows in envelopes that never line up with the address.

PREMADERCI
(pree muh dayr' chi)

n. The act of saying goodbye to someone, then running into him again moments later (usually accompanied by a lame quip such as "you following me?").

PREMAIL
(pree' mayl)

n. Mail that is placed behind the visor in the car and left for several months before it is finally sent.

PRETZALINE
(pret sah leen')

n. The salt deposit at the bottom of a bag of pretzels.

PRIMPO
(prim' po)

n. A person who passes a mirror then has to step back, presumably to reassure himself he still exists.

P-SPOT
(pee' spaht)

n. The area directly above the urinal in public restrooms that men stare at, knowing a glance in any other direction would arouse suspicion.

PULPID
(puhl' pid)

n. A kid who enjoys the carton more than the item that came in it.

PULPULARITY
(puhl pyew lahr' ih tee)

n. Molecular property of newspaper clippings that allows them to tear evenly north to south but jaggedly east to west.

PUNTIFICATE

(puhn tih' fih kayt)

v. To try to predict in what direction a football will bounce.

PUPSQUEAK
(puhp' skweek)

n. The sound a yawning dog emits when it opens its mouth too wide.

RAMPRIOT
(ramp' ry uht)

n. Free-for-all that erupts as soon as the stewardess utters the phrase "please remain in your seats until the plane has come to a complete stop."

RELED
(ree led')

v. To reset all the digital clocks in the household following a power failure.

ROEBINKS
(roh' binks)

n. Those mysterious chimes you always hear in department stores.

ROHRSHIRT
(roar' shurt)

n. A shirt with an ink stain on the pocket.

RUBBAGE
(ruh' bij)

n. Large pieces of truck tire found on the side of the road.

SCHWIGGLE
(shwi' gul)

n. The amusing rotation of one's bottom while sharpening a pencil.

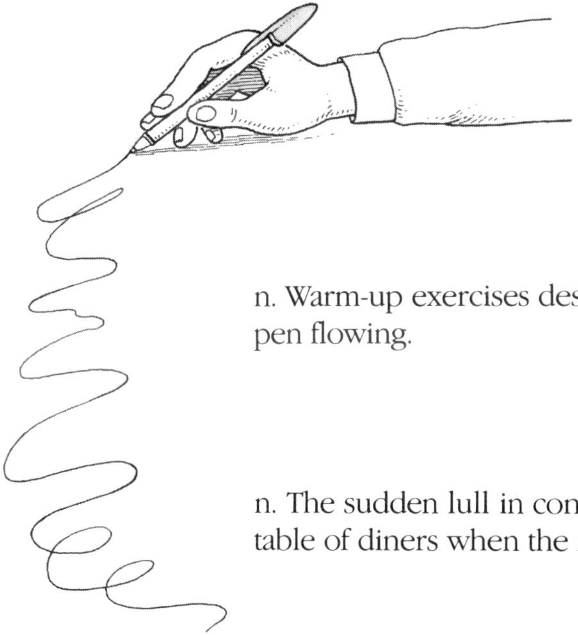

SCRIBBLICS
(skrib' bliks)

n. Warm-up exercises designed to get the ink in a pen flowing.

SERVELENCE
(surv' lents)

n. The sudden lull in conversation that occurs at a table of diners when the food is served.

SHOCKLET

(shahk' lit)

n. The seldom-used third hole on an electrical outlet.

74

sho

SHUZMA

(shuhz' muh)

n. The portion of window cleaner that the spray tube can no longer reach.

SLOPWEAVER
(slahp' wee vuhr)

n. Someone who has mastered the art of repositioning the food on his plate to give the appearance of having consumed a good portion of it.

SLOTTERY AND VENDICATION
(slot' er ee and ven' di kay shun)

n. A public misdemeanor in which a person gambles on a vending machine, loses, and tries to exact revenge by kicking it.

SLURCH
(slerch)

n. The combination "ouch" and slurping noise one makes when eyeing someone else's bad sunburn.

SNACKMOSPHERE
(snak' moh sfeer)

n. The empty but explosive layer of air at the top of a potato chip bag.

SNARGLE
(snar' gul)

v. To lessen the visual impact of a horror movie by filtering it through one's fingers.

SNUGGAGE
(snuh' gaj)

n. The act of retying both shoestrings when only one needed it.

SOMNAMBAPOLOGIST
(som nam ba pol' uh jist)

n. Person too polite to admit he was sleeping even when awakened at three in the morning.

SPAGELLUM
(spa gel' um)

n. The loose strand on each forkful of spaghetti that beats one about the chin and whiskers.

SPOOD
(spewd)

n. Flat wooden "spoon" that accompanies ice cream cups.

SPROUT LINES
(sprowt lynz)

n. Visible lines at the bottom of trouser legs where the hems have been let down.

SPUDRUBBLE
(spud' rubb uhl)

n. Unclaimed french fries at the bottom of a fast food bag.

SQUAFFELS
(skwa' felz)

n. The individual squares comprising a waffle.

SQUANDERPRINT
(skwan' duhr print)

n. Directions that try to make you use up a product faster than you normally would. (Ex.: Apply shampoo. Lather. Rinse. Repeat.)

SQUATFLECTION

(skwat' flek shun)

n. The distorted reflection in a car window that makes you resemble a midget wrestler.

SQUATIC DIVERSION
(skwa' tik dy vur' zhun)

n. Any pretended activity that commands a dog owner's attention while the dog relieves itself on a neighbor's lawn.

SQUIGGER
(skwig' uhr)

n. A cherry tomato that explodes upon contact with a fork.

SUBATOMIC TOASTICLES
(sub ah tom' ik toh' stik uhlz)

n. Tiny fragments of toast left behind in the butter.

TABLE SNORKELING

(tay' bul snawrk' ling)

n. Frantic gesticulations when one bites into hot food and has to take in air to cool it off.

TELLETIQUETTE

(tel et' ih ket)

n. The polite distance kept by one person behind another at an automatic teller machine (so as not to be suspected of trying to glimpse that person's secret code).

TELOUSTIC
(tel oo' stik)

adj. The tendency for people to shout into the phone when calling long distance.

TESTLICE
(test' lys)

n. Those tiny bugs that invade your hair when you're taking an exam.

TOILET TOUPEE
(toy' lit too pay')

n. Any shag carpet toilet cover that causes the lid to become top - heavy, thus creating endless annoyance to male users.

TOOLCENTRIC
(tewl sen' trik)

adj. Describes any tool that, when dropped, rolls to the exact center of the car's underside.

TRIDECKPICK

(try dek' pik)

n. A miniature sword or similar device used to hold a sandwich together.

TUBSWIZZLE

(tub' swih zuhl)

v. To slide oneself back and forth in the bathtub in order to mix the too hot water with the cooler water.

TURFIGEE AND PEDIGEE
(ter' fih jee and ped' ih jee)

n. The two extreme target points of a rotary lawn sprinkler, TURFIGEE being the safest point at which to walk past, PEDIGEE being the most dangerous.

TWINKIDUE
(twin' kee dew)

n. The residue on the inside of the wrapper that every junk food addict eventually gets to.

UCLIPSE
(yew' klips)

n. The dangerous arc into another lane made by drivers just before executing a turn.

UMBILINKUS
(uhm bih link' us)

n. The tiny appendage at the end of a link sausage.

UMBRACE
(uhm' brays)

n. The small strap that holds an umbrella in place.

UNDERHOODIST
(un dur hood' ist)

n. A service station attendant with a genius for locating hood latches.

UNFARE
(un fayr')

n. The dollar you owe the cab driver before you've even moved a foot.

UNIPEA
(yew' ni pee)

n. A peanut with only one compartment.

VACATION ELBOW
(vay kay' shun el' bo)

n. A condition that suddenly develops in a father's arm during a vacation trip that allows him to reach out and slap you from incredible distances.

VEGELUDES
(vej' eh loodz)

n. Individual peas or kernels of corn that you end up chasing all over the plate.

VENDOMETRIC
(ven doh meh' trik)

n. A person who inserts his change in a vending machine according to size (dimes, nickels, quarters).

VENDOVALUEIST
(ven doh val' yew ist)

n. A person who inserts his change according to value (nickels, dimes, quarters).

VOITLOCK
(voyt' lok)

n. When the basketball gets lodged between the rim and the backboard.

WAFTIC
(wahf' tik)

adj. Describes any person in whose direction campfire or barbeque smoke always blows.

WERDLE

(wurd' uhl)

v. To lean over the edge of a train or subway platform in search of the oncoming vehicle. WERDLEMASS (n.)—an entire group of people leaning over a train or subway platform.

WISKAGE
(wis' kaj)

n. The gravitational property that causes clothes to stick to the outside of the drum after the spin cycle.

WOOWAD
(wew' wad)

n. Giant clumps of stuck-together rice served at Chinese restaurants.

XEROXPOX
(zee' roks poks)

n. Skin disease of copier paper, characterized by the appearance of large black powdery blotches.

YOTATE
(yoh' tayt)

v. To allow a yo-yo to unwind itself.

ZEBRALANE
(zee' bruh layn)

n. The striped area between the interstate and the turnoff lane where cars go when drivers can't decide what to do next.

ZEEPT
(zeept)

n. The accumulation of dead insects around an electric bug fryer.

ZERBLOT
(zur' blaht)

n. The last kid picked in any neighborhood sporting event.

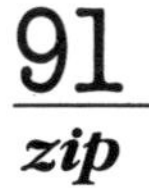

ZIPCUFFED
(zip' cuft)

v. To be trapped in one's trousers by a faulty zipper.

How to Use Your Sniglets Videodisc

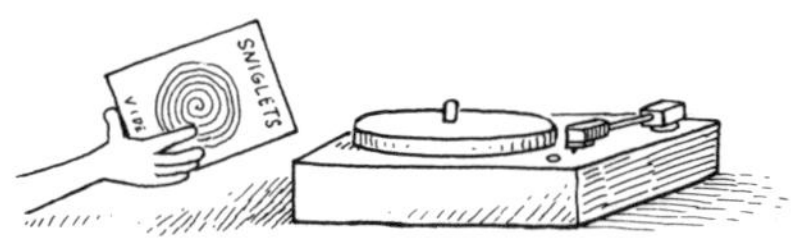

1. Remove disc along dotted line and place on any turntable.

2. Make sure turntable is plugged into electrical outlet.

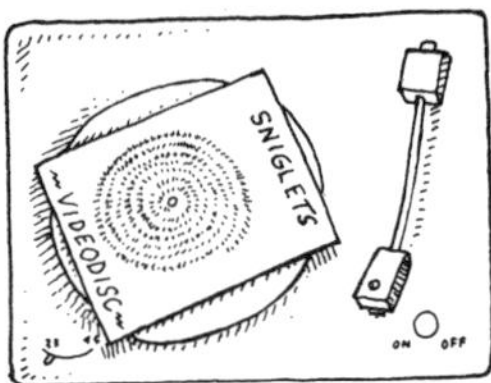

3. Using finger, rotate platter of turntable in a counterclockwise direction. View sniglets.

4. When you have completed viewing the sniglets, you may rewind the disc by rotating it in the opposite direction.

Videodisc

ARG (AUDIO RETINAL GYRATION) (ay ahr gee) v. To move the head in a circular fashion while attempting to read a rotating record label.

DASHBLAST (dash'blast) n. The headsplitting change in decibel levels when a car tape is removed and the radio comes on.

RADIOLIMBO (ray dee oh lim'boh) n. Long expanses of interstate highway where it is impossible to pick up any radio broadcasts except livestock reports.

SILICANAPE (sih lih kan'uh pay) n. The little bag of silica gel found among stereo parts marked "Do Not Eat."

OFFICIAL SNIGLETS ENTRY BLANK

Dear Rich:

Here's my contribution to the English language. I'm sure it's as good as yours:

____

____

____

____

____

Sincerely,

(name) ______________________________

(street address) ______________________________

(city, state, zip code) ______________________________

Idiot
Box

SNIGLETS
P.O. Box 2350
Hollywood, CA 90078

UNEXPLAINED SNIGLETS OF THE UNIVERSE

RICH HALL & FRIENDS

Illustrated by Arnie Ten

ALFRED HITCHCOOKING *(al' fred hich' cooh king)*
v. Continuously stabbing at a block of frozen vegetables to make them cook faster.

UNEXPLAINED SNIGLETS OF THE UNIVERSE

(snig' lit):

any word that doesn't appear in the dictionary, but should

Collier Books • Macmillan Publishing Company • New York

Collier Macmillan Publishers • London

"Not Necessarily the News," a production of Not the Network Company, Inc., in association with Moffitt-Lee Productions, is produced by John Moffitt and co-produced by Pat Tourk Lee.

Macmillan Publishing Company
866 Third Avenue, New York, N.Y. 10022
Collier Macmillan Canada, Inc.

Library of Congress Cataloging-in-Publication Data
Hall, Rich, 1954–
Unexplained sniglets of the universe
1. Words, New—English—Anecdotes, facetiae, satire, etc.—
2. Vocabulary—Anecdotes, facetiae, satire, etc.
I. Title.
PN6231.W64H34 1986 428.1′0207
85-23179
ISBN 0-02-040400-X (pbk.)

10 9 8 7 6 5 4 3 2

Designed by Antler & Baldwin, Inc.
PRINTED IN THE UNITED STATES OF AMERICA

To Darby

CONTRIBUTORS

Marc Allen Mel Abveg Jim Bailey Matt Besterman Mike Bivens Connie Boyd Gene Brown Dean Burgess Drew Butler Debbie Cantrell Lynn Carlson Al Causey Keith Cerasoli Andrew Chatterson Derek Clawson John C. Coble Dave Coey Matthew Cordo Donald Cililla Brian Cullinan Steven Cortina Tyler Deans Perry Dennis Stephen Dyer Lynn and Joel Eskin Linda Felten Michael Francisco Joe Garagiola Alex Gastgeb Todd Gerber Lou Gershenson David Gross Jim Grybowski **Rich Hall** Pat Hamlett Mack Hendricks Teresa Holik Tom Huber Geof Huth Eric Johnston Neal Katz John D. Kellog Nick Kosan Jr. Bill Kraft Kris Kranig Don Kinzel Teddy Kruljac Mike Kundak Michael Laird Jack Laurie Chris Leavell Chris Levi Dean Lewis Patrick Leyba Ray and Lisa Daniele Lussier Liz Matheny Ryan Maynes Karen Meyer Tom Mikita Bob Myles Gary Muldoon Ryan Nelson Dave Newman Mike O'Shea Kris Parker Mike Payne David Perazzo Ken Post Shane Poulter Jeff Radoicic Harry Ralston Brian Raslawski Carol Reichiert Paula Reisinger John Rhodes Tony Roberti David Robertson Richard Rosalia Jim Rosen Tom Russell Eric Saphire Ev Schafer Frank Scaldone Tony Scacifero Cindy Seglowich Steve Serra Ira Shain Jonathan Shandell Mike Siggins Jim Sippola Cheryl Six Stephanie Snow Brian Stewart Ross Storm Scott Strent Tim Thomas Matt Thompson Jonathan Tully Florence Tummolo Richard Vickroy John Wiening Mary Weiss Adert Welkin Robert J. Woodhead L. N. Yarbrough Chris Zarcone Vincent Zedler

CONTENTS

UNEXPLAINED SNIGLETS OF THE UNIVERSE

ACELLOYELLOS
(a sel' oh yel' oz)

n. People who speed through caution lights.

AGE OF CLAUSABILITY
(ayj' uv klaw' za bil' ih tee)

n. The point at which we stop believing in Santa.

AIRCAPPED
(ayr' capt)

v. To be temporarily crippled when the airplane passenger in front of you drives his seat back into your knees.

AIRPUNT

(ayr' punt)

n. Any of a series of kicks that advances one's baggage toward the airport counter.

ALFALFABET

(al fal' fuh bet)

n. Backward letters used only on clubhouse doors.

ALFRED HITCHCOOKING
(al' fred hich' cooh king)

v. Continuously stabbing at a block of frozen vegetables to make them cook faster.

ANANANANY
(an a na' na nee)

n. The inability to stop spelling the word "banana" once you've started.

ANAFONDICS
(an a fon' diks)

n. Exercising to a workout album at 16 RPM.

APPLAFLAMMAPHOBIA
(ap la flam uh fo' bee uh)

n. Fear that upon departing for vacation, you've left an appliance on that will burn the house to the ground.

AQUACOUSTICS
(ak wa koo' stiks)

n. Sound waves in the bathroom that enable anyone to sing on key.*

ASPIRBAYERPERPAIR-PERFECTION
(as pur bayr' pur payr' pur fek' shun)

n. The ability to always extract *exactly* two headache tablets from the bottle.

ASTEREXASPER
(as tuhr eggs as' pur)

n. An asterisk with no corresponding footnote.

n. Experience of waking up on New Year's Day and wondering how much of a fool you made of yourself.

AWSLICE
(aww' slice)

n. The first slice of a wedding cake. The one which ruins the design and causes everyone to sigh.

AZUGOS
(as' you goes)

n. Items to be carried upstairs by the next ascending person.

BARFIUM
(bar' fee um)

n. The horrible smelling cleanser they mop down school corridors with.

BACKIN-MYDAY ACT OF 1901
(bak' in my' day akt uv nein' teen oh wun')

n. Law created in the early part of the twentieth century which made it mandatory to build schools at least 20 miles away from all future grandfathers.

BALLYBUSTER
(bal' lee bus tur)

n. A pinball machine with one dead flipper.

BARBALYSIS
(bar ba' lih sis)

n. Condition that arises from having to keep your head motionless while getting a haircut.

BARCUUMING
(bar' ku ming)

v. Using the family dog to remove the crumbs that have dropped to the floor.

BEVAMIRAGE
(bev' uh mih rahj)

n. Deceiving black ring around the bottom of a two-liter soda bottle.

BLISTERPEG
(blys' tur peg)

n. The irritating part of a thong or flip flop that holds your foot on.

BLOG
(blahg)

n. Overly generous deposits of fish food floating at the top of an aquarium.

BLOSSOR
(blos' er)

n. Unique "winged" hairstyle achieved after wearing a baseball cap for several hours.

BROOP
(broop)

n. The useless pocket on a pajama top.

BURGATORY
(ber' ga tawr ee)

n. The place where unsold burgers go when the stand shuts down for the night.

BUTTRAS
(but' ruhs)

n. Those small buttons in a plastic bag that accompany finer clothing.

CANTWITIONIST
(kan twi' shun ist)

n. Person who manually "rushes" the lid on an electric can opener.

CARPILLARY ACTION
(kar' pih ler ee ak' shun)

n. Property that enables water to move up a windshield when the vehicle is in motion.

CHEDDARBLISTER

(ched' ur blihs tur)

n. The bubble formed when making a grilled cheese sandwich.

CHOCOZIPPER

(chok' oh zip ur)

n. The tab that releases a Hershey's Kiss.

CHOCTASY

(chok' ta see)

n. The joy of discovering a second layer of chocolates underneath the first.

CHRONESIA

(kron ee' zyuh)

n. The tendency not to know the time when asked, even though you've just checked your watch.

CINEDRAFT

(sin' uh draft)

n. The mysterious rush of air that sucks your money into the ticket window at the movie theater.

CINEPLEGIC

(sih neh plee' jik)

n. A person whose foot has temporarily lost circulation from being wedged between theater seats.

CIRCUMVACULATE
(sur kum vak' yew layt)

v. To remain stationary while vacuuming in a circle around oneself.

COINOPHONY
(koy' nah foh nee)

n. Annoying pocket concerts conducted by people who like to jingle keys and change, often accompanied by a rocking motion.

COMEONDOWNS
(kum on downz')

n. Depression resulting from knowing all the answers to a game show while confined in your living room.

CORNISECTION
(kor' nih sek shun)

n. The systematic consumption of candy corn by sections, first biting off the white zone, then the orange zone, then the yellow zone.

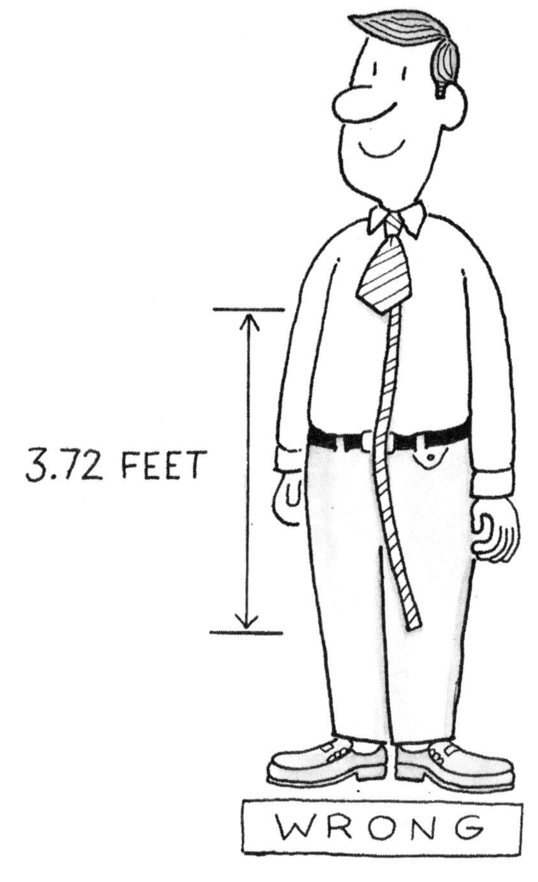
3.72 FEET
WRONG

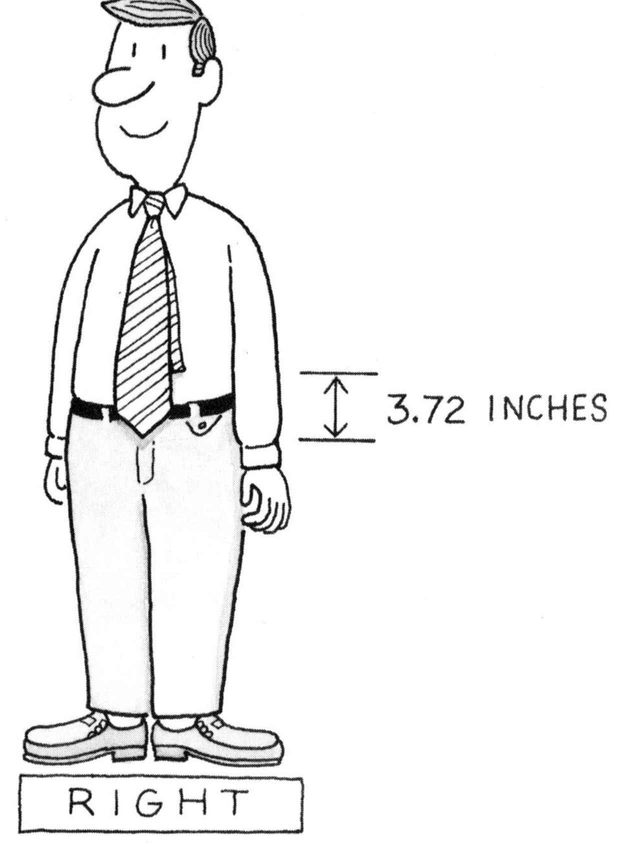
3.72 INCHES
RIGHT

CRAVAMETER
(kra' va mih tur)

n. 3.72 inches, the proper distance between the ends of a tied tie.

CROONO EN FLAGRANTE
(krew' noh on fla grahn' tay)

v. To be caught singing to the muzak when the secretary takes you off hold.

CRUSTADJUSTER
(krus' ta jus tur)

n. The "light-dark" knob on a toaster that makes you think you're in control.

CUBESTACLE

(kewb' stack ul)

n. A person who, no matter where he stands, gets in the way of someone shooting pool.

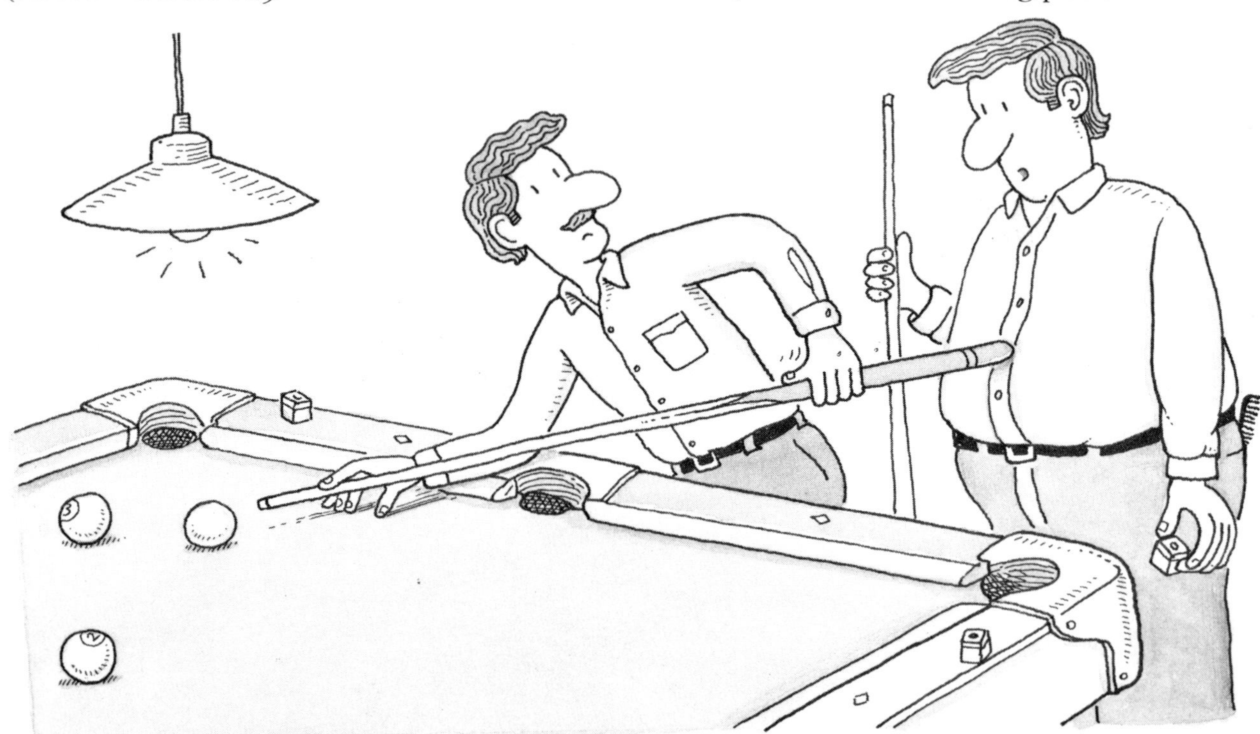

CUFFLATCH
(kuf' lach)

v. To grasp the edge of one's sleeve to keep it from slithering up the arm while pulling on a sport jacket.

CURDUNDANCY
(kur dun' dan see)

n. The big deal of opening and closing the theater curtains between preview and feature in movie theaters, presumably to help justify the five-dollar admission.

CURODDS
(kur' ohds)

n. The adhesive bandages at the bottom of the box designed for extremely unusual injuries.

DENNIDIOTS
(den id' ee uts)

n. People who actually fill out those "How-was-the-service" exams on the backs of restaurant checks.

DIAGONERD
(dy ag' oh nurd)

n. Person who angles his car across two spaces to keep people from parking too close.

DUDOUT
(dud' owt)

n. Condition of having consumed all of one's snack bar items before the movie even started.

DÜNKEN HÄCKEN
(dun' kin ha' kin)

n. Violent coughing attack brought on by inhaling the powdered sugar on a doughnut.

ECTOLACTO
(ek toh lak' toh)

n. That curtain of milk that runs down the outside of the glass when you try to pour it into the cereal bowl.

EGGORY
(eg' er ee)

n. The part of the fridge that holds the eggs.

ELEMENO
(LMNO)

n. The centermost letter in the alphabet. The one that reduces it from twenty-six characters to twenty-three.

ESSOASSO

(es oh as' oh)

n. A person who cuts through a service station to avoid a red light.

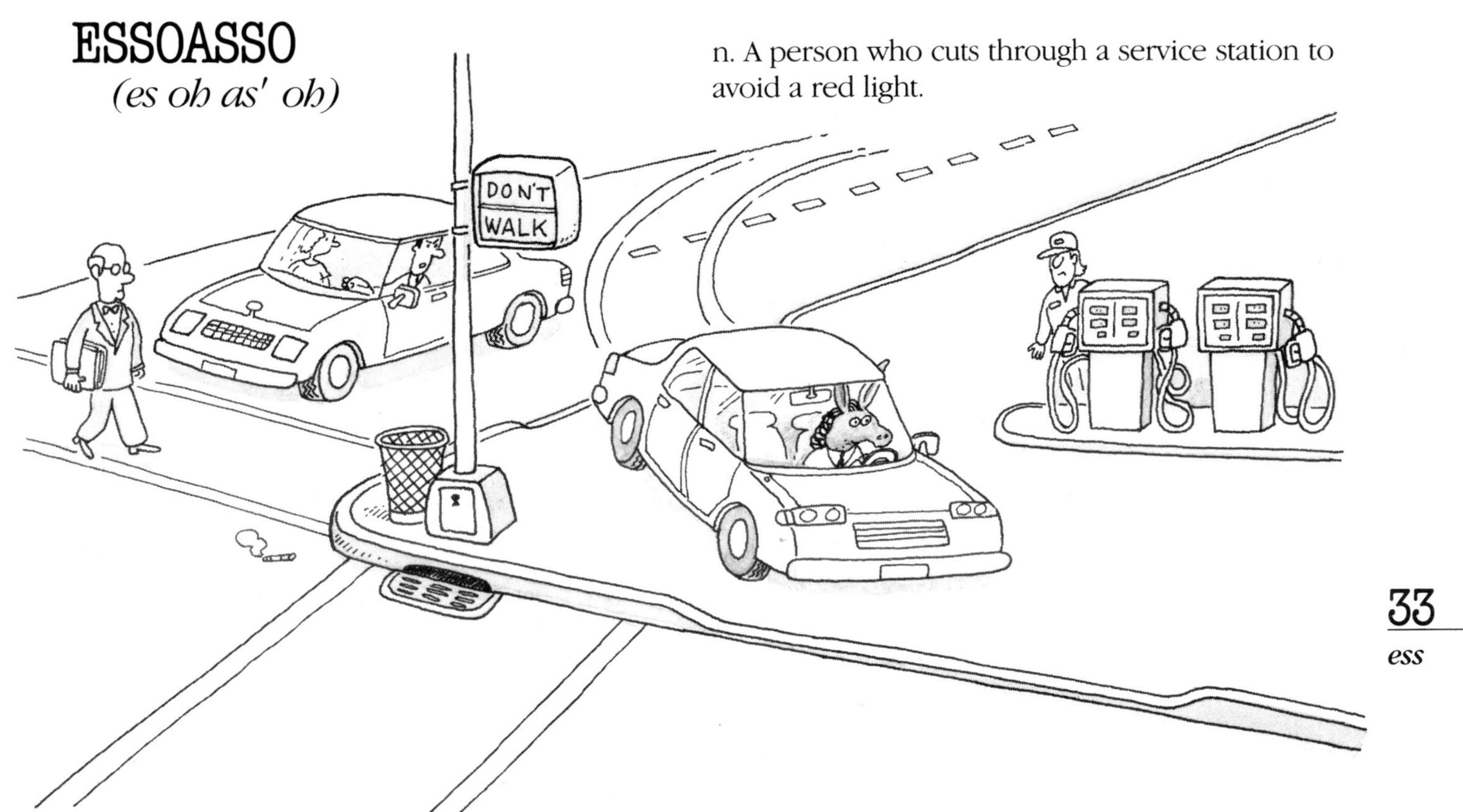

EXCESS BUNNERAGE
(eks' es bun' ur aj)

adj. When the buns at a cookout come in eight packs and the hot dogs in sixes.

EXCESS WIENERAGE
(eks' es wee' nur aj)

adj. When the buns come in eight packs and the hot dogs in twelve. (See also **FRANQUILIZED**.)

EX-O-VAC
(ex' oh vak)

n. The third battery in a "buy two get one free" package that is useless unless you buy a second pack.

FALOOTER
(fa lew' tur)

n. The rope running through a menu that lets you know you're at a fancy restaurant.

FARRELPHOBIA
(fayr el foh' bee yuh)

n. Fear of being approached by several dozen waiters singing, "Happy Birthday."

FEASERS
(fee' zurz)

n. The racing stripes on tennis shoes that fool kids into thinking they can run faster.

FIGFORCE
(fig' faurs)

n. Mysterious magnetic force that holds two or more Fig Newtons together.

FIRSSUE
(fur' shew)

n. The lead tissue. The one that gets all the others going.

FLEABAGE
(flee' baj)

n. Excess of flea collar that has to be cut off.

FOOMLET
(foom' lit)

n. The bathroom towel you're not allowed to use because it's marked "guest," and guests don't use because who wants to be the first person to mess it up?

FOOPERS

(foo' perz)

n. Passers-by at restaurant windows who stop to watch you eat.

FRANQUILIZED
(frank' wil ized)

adj. When, by some miracle, you have an equal number of buns and wieners at a cookout.

FUTILITY INFIELDER
(few til' ih tee in' feel dur)

n. One who tries to stop grounders by throwing his glove at them.

GARBPACTION
(garb pak' shun)

v. The act of cramming just one more item into a garbage can to avoid emptying it.

GENTREA
(jen' tree uh)

n. The small area of the windshield beneath the steering wheel used by elderly drivers.

GEOUCH

(jee' owch)

n. The sharp rock one always finds directly beneath his sleeping bag.

GREEPERS
(greep' ers)

n. People who walk up the down escalator in an attempt to appear motionless.

GUNKOLEUM
(gun koh' lee yum)

n. The horrible black paste that car manufacturers smear under car seats.

GYMBOLS
(jim' bolz)

n. Those lines and markings on a gym floor that have no purpose whatsoever.

HALASKA
(ha las' kuh)

n. The boxed area on a U.S. map where our 49th and 50th states are located.

HEMOPLUGS
(hee' moh plugz)

n. Small pieces of toilet paper applied to shaving wounds.

HIGHYIMES
(hi' yimes)

n. Those 800 number operators who threaten to return at the end of the magazine subscription commercial to "tell you how to receive your free gift."

HOOPTOOTS
(hoop' tewts)

n. Strange bugle sounds at basketball games, the source of which no one seems to be able to identify.

WELCOME
to THE MALL
YOU
ARE
HERE
DIRECTORY
BABY'S
STORE
I ♥
THE
MALL
I ♥
THE
MALL

42

idi

IDIOLOCATION
(yd' ee oh low kay' shun)

n. The spot on the shopping mall map marked, "you are here."

ILLUMINOT
(il ew' mih naht)

n. Device in airplane bathrooms that won't let the light come on until you lock the door.

IMPASSENGERS
(im pas' enj urz)

n. Two people, one inside the car, one outside, negating each other's actions while trying to unlock the door.

44
ine

INELVITABLE

(in el' vih tuh bul)

adj. The uncanny ability of a band in old Elvis Presley movies to materialize from nowhere whenever Elvis begins to sing.

INKNITION

(ink nih' shun)

n. The metal clicker at the top of a cheap ball point pen that: a) puts it into operation and b) is also perfect for driving substitute teachers crazy.

INNINGFRINGEMENT

(in ning frinj' ment)

n. The warning near the end of a baseball broadcast that says you better not try to start your own station and "rebroadcast the accounts and descriptions of this game."

JAVAJETSAM

(ja va jet' sum)

n. Washed ashore coffee grounds on the rim of the cup.

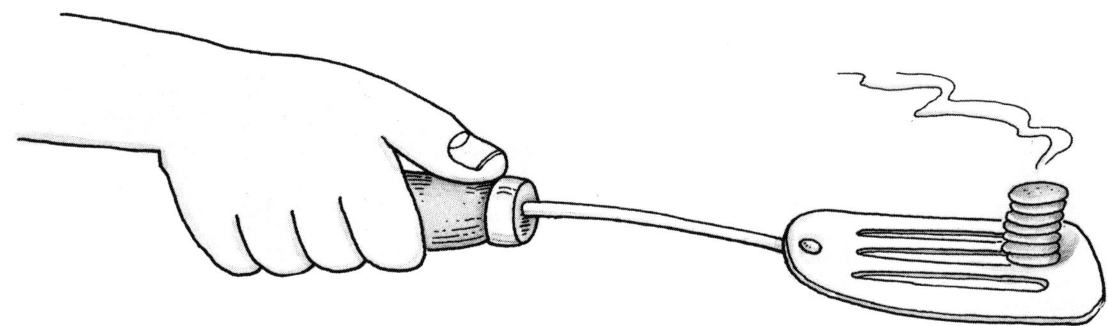

JEMIMITES

(je my' myts)

n. Extremely tiny pancakes formed from the batter that fell off the ladle.

JUJUSPECTION
(joo' joo spek shun)

v. Holding a jujube up to the cinema screen in order to determine its color.

KEYLONIUS
(key loan' ee us)

adj. The slight trace of criminality one feels when having his keys duplicated.

LEXICAVES
(leks' ih kayvz)

n. Indentations on the side of a dictionary.

LEXPLEXED
(leks' plekst)

adj. Unable to find the correct spelling for a word in the dictionary because you don't know how to spell it.

LIGS
(ligz)

n. The two small metal tabs that hold an Ace bandage in place.

LINENARCTICA
(lin en ark' tik uh)

n. The corner of the bed that is impossible to reach when putting on new sheets.

LINTHLYPTUS
(lin tu lip' tus)

n. Any cough drop found in one's pocket after a long period of time.

LITMUSLOAD
(lit' mus lode)

n. Any washload that comes out the color of the one item that faded.

MAGLERK
(mag' lurk)

n. Ingenious wedge made in a coffee lid to facilitate safe consumption while driving.

MALTIGO
(mahl' tih go)

n. Temporary state of confusion upon exiting a store in a mall and not remembering which direction one entered by.

MANUMULCHING
(man' yew mul ching)

v. Transporting leaves by sandwiching them between one hand and the rake.

MARGRANE
(mar' grayn)

n. The blinding pain from drinking Margarita slush too quickly.

MAYTAG MASSAGE
(may' tag muh sahj')

n. The momentary thrill experienced while sitting on a washer as it launches into the spin cycle.

McNERTIA
(mak nur' sha)

n. Malaise that prevents a McDonald's employee from filling your order too quickly, or correctly.

MEDIPEEP
(meh' dee peep)

n. Uncontrollable urge to look inside a host's bathroom cabinet to see what kind of afflictions he suffers from.

MEGANEGABAR
(meg uh neg' uh bar)

n. The line you draw across the "amount" section of a check to prevent people from adding, "and a million dollars."

MEMOMIMICRY
(mem oh mim' ih kree)

n. The brief lapse in a phone conversation where you pretend to be getting a pencil to write down an important message.

MEMOSPHERE
(meh' moh sfeer)

n. The part of the sky one searches when trying to recall something in the past.

MINIBLURB
(mih' nee blerb)

n. That useless piece of information about the author found on the back of a book.

MINNIE PEARL VISION

(mih' nee perl' vizh' un)

n. Trying to envision how a pair of drugstore sunglasses will look on you without the huge tag hanging from them.

MINUTATER

(min'u tay tur)

n. The smallest french fry in the bag. (See also **POTENTATER**, the largest french fry in the bag.)

MIRRORCIDE

(mi' rawr side)

n. Leading cause of death among finches and parakeets.

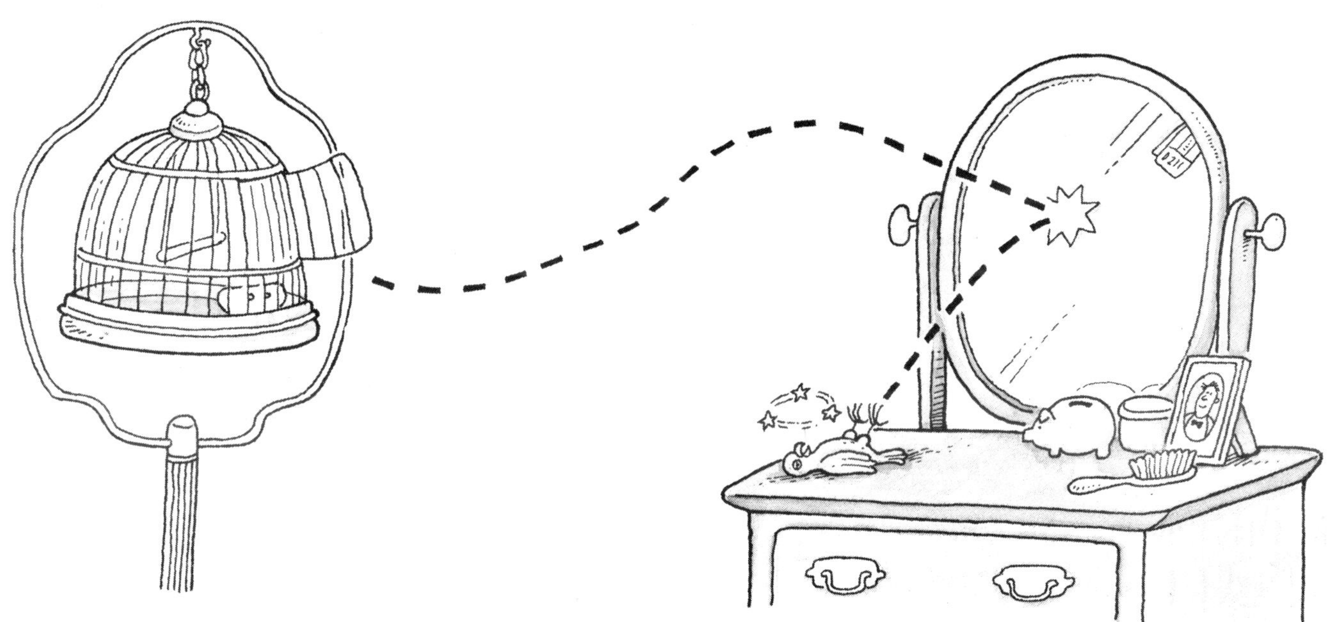

MISSPITS
(mis' spitz)

n. Albino watermelon seeds.

MOLOTOV CARTAIL
(mah' lah tav kar' tayl)

n. Any service station towel used in place of a gas cap.

MOMMENOIA
(mom muh noy' ah)

n. Fear that the dentist or doctor will barge in and catch you playing with his equipment.

MUGPUDDLES
(mug' pud ulz)

n. Small bodies of water that collect on upturned mugs in the dishwasher.

NICAMEASLES
(nik' a mee zulz)

n. Brown dots on the front of a ballplayer's uniform from spitting tobacco and missing.

NINKER
(nin' kur)

n. Any utensil that positions itself inside a drawer to prevent the drawer from opening.

NITVWIT
(nit' vwit)

n. Any person who can't find reverse gear in a Volkswagen.

NOUGALICITY
(noo ga lis' ih tee)

n. Degree to which a Snickers bar will stretch before the caramel snaps.

NOZZLOP

(noz' zlop)

n. To look into a garden hose to see if the water is coming.

NUTRASECOND
(new' truh sek und)

n. The few seconds of pleasure before the after-taste of a diet drink sets in.

NUTTONBUTTON
(nut'n' but'n)

n. The device at intersections marked, "push to cross."

ORQO
(oar' ko)

n. The small bar that turns an "O" into a "Q." (Not to be confused with the Arqo which is the bar that turns an "R" into a drugstore.)

PARSLEYVANIA
(par slee vay' nyuh)

n. The place where all the fancy restaurant garnish that is never eaten comes from.

PASTAPLEGIC
(pas tuh plee' jik)

n. Person who's eaten so much spaghetti he can't move.

PAYFALL
(pay' fal)

n. The phone booth sound that tricks you into thinking your coin accidentally returned.

PEAMORPHO
(pee mor' foh)

n. The peanut butter that escapes through the holes to the other side of the cracker.

PEEPOLA
(pee poe' luh)

n. The gap in the dressing room curtain that can never be completely closed.

PENCICOPTER

(pen' sih kop tur)

n. Classroom invention fashioned from a pencil and a ruler during periods of extreme boredom.

PEPSILLUVIUM
(pep sil lew' vee yum)

n. The tiny amount of cola that escapes when you push a straw through the lid of a soft drink.

PERCALEVATE
(pur kayl' eh vate)

v. To levitate oneself while trying to straighten out the sheets underneath.

PLACEBASE
(pla see' bays)

n. Any item used as a base in a baseball game during an equipment shortage, such as a rock or large turtle.

POPTROOPERS
(pahp' trew purz)

n. Kernels that leap over the side of the container onto the counter when popcorn is being purchased.

POTENTATER
(poh' ten tay tur)

n. The largest french fry in the bag. (See also **MINUTATER**, the smallest french fry in the bag.)

PREMALOOMA
(prem a loo' ma)

n. Any piece of aluminum foil that comes off the roll looking like the state of Nevada.

PULPSQULPGULP
(pulp' skulp gulp)

v. To slurp the grapefruit juice straight from the bowl it's served in and abandon all civility.

PURCILIOUS
(per sil' ee us)

adj. The manner in which a man holds his wife's pocketbook in public, as if it contained some odious matter.

PYRAMONSTER
(pie' ruh mon stur)

n. That thing with one big eye on the back of a dollar bill.

QUADRIPHOBIA
(kwa dri foh' bee yuh)

n. Fear of approaching a four-way stop sign and not knowing "who goes next."

RECOGILOG
(re kog' ih log)

n. The list inside of a library book that you always check to see if you recognize anyone else who wasted time reading it.

REMOTANT
(ree moh' tant)

n. Any alien creature who suddenly appears in the background of a news or feature report.

RETINUS PIGMENTOASTUS
(reh' tih nus pig men tos' tus)

n. Condition of being misled by the tinted window on a toaster oven into thinking something is "done."

REYULERATE
(re yew' lur ayt)

v. To reposition Christmas tree lights so no two of the same colors are beside each other.

RINGS OF RATH AND KAHN
(ringz' uhv rath' and cahn')

n. The mysterious red rings encircling sliced baloney.

ROGERLAND

(rah' jer land)

n. The netherworld from which highway patrolmen suddenly materialize.

ROTOCORONETIC
(roh toh cah roh net' ik)

n. A person who eats corn on the cob in an up and down or "column" style. (See also **SMITHCORONETIC**.)

RUMPHUMP
(rump' bump)

n. The seat on the school bus directly over the rear wheel.

SCHLITZSTOP
(schlits' stop)

n. The one player in amateur softball games who always thinks he can handle his position and a beer at the same time.

SCORBAGE
(skor' bahj)

n. Wadded up trash hurled toward the wastebasket from across the room.

SCOTCHROTOR
(skoch' roh tur)

n. The wheel left behind when all the cellophane tape is used up.

SECOND OILPINION [TO GET A]
(seh'cund oyl pin' yun)

v. Checking a dipstick, wiping it off, then *rechecking* because you never "trust" it the first time.

SHOWERSHROUD

(show' ur shrowd)

n. Those hotel shower curtains that inexplicably wrap themselves around you while you shower.

SIZZLAGE
(siz' lidge)

n. The amount of skin one is willing to sacrifice while testing an iron to make sure it won't burn one's shirt.

SKIVLINES
(skiv' lynz)

n. The red or blue lines around jockey shorts that make them resemble fine China.

SLOANTIME
(sloun' tym)

n. The difference between real time and the time displayed atop the bank.

SLOOVERS
(sloo' vurz)

n. Remnants of soap too small to use, but too big to throw away.

SLOVERTURE
(slow' vur chur)

n. The distorted music which begins every educational movie.

SMITHCORONETIC
(smith cah roh net' ik)

n. A person who eats corn on the cob in a left to right or "typewriter" style. (See also **ROTOCORONETIC**.)

SMOKEYPOKEY
(smoh kee poh' kee)

n. Inertia that overcomes cars when they suddenly encounter a highway patrolman.

SMOOK
(smewk)

n. The flimsy paper stretched across the examining table at a doctor's office.

SMUGSTICKER
(smug' stih kur)

n. The price tag that normally intelligent people leave on their new car window for months.

SNABBLE
(sna' bul)

v. To attempt to use a sniglet while playing Scrabble.

SPUMPSPEED

(spump' speed)

n. The velocity achieved between speed bumps before having to slow down again.

SQUINCHOOING

(skwin chew' ing)

v. Staring up at the sun to expedite a sneeze.

STOPTIONAL

(stop' shun ul)

n. Any stop sign in the middle of nowhere that no one pays attention to.

SUBWAY SURFERS

(sub' way sur' furz)

n. People on public transportation with the uncanny ability to maintain perfect balance without using the straps.

SUDSORIAN CALENDAR

(sudz oar' ee an ka' len dur)

n. Calendar used on soap operas which allows one day's events to be stretched over a three-week period.

SUZMOSIS
(suz moh' sis)

n. Mysterious disappearance of dishwater even when the sink is stopped airtight.

SWURLEE
(swer' lee)

n. A playground swing wrapped impossibly out of reach.

T-RATION
(tee' ra shun)

v. To use less and less toilet paper as one nears the end of the roll.

TACANGLE
(tak' ang ul)

n. The position of one's head while biting into a taco.

TATERCRATER
(tay' tur kray' tur)

n. Hole dug in mashed potatoes to keep the gravy in.

TELEVELOCITY
(teh leh veh la' sih tee)

n. The speed at which one tries to reach the phone before the answering machine comes on.

TERMA HELPER
(ter' ma hel' pur)

n. The extra verbiage one uses to stretch a 600-word essay to the required 1000.

TEXAS SEE-SAW MASSACRE
(teks' us see' saw mas' uh kur)

n. When the other person bails off a teeter-totter slamming you to the ground.

THREEK
(threek)

n. A fork with a bent tine.

THRUB

(thrub)

n. The small web of skin between the thumb and index finger that makes us 0.0005% amphibian.

TOASTIPHOBIA

(toh stihfoh' bee yuh)

n. Fear of putting a fork in the toaster even when it is unplugged because, somehow, the toaster "remembers."

TODLITTER
(tod' lit ur)

n. Food debris under a high chair following an attempted feeding.

TRUFITTI
(truh fee' tee)

n. Washing instructions found on the backs of dirty trucks.

TUBLOIDS
(tubb' loydz)

n. Any periodical reserved for bathroom readings.

TUPPERWARP
(tuh' pur warp)

n. Condition of Tupperware left in the microwave too long.

UHFLAW
(yu' flaw)

n. The one television tuned to a different channel in the bank of televisions at the appliance store.

ULTIMATO
(ul tih may' toe)

n. The choice of eating your vegetables or going to bed without supper.

UMBROGLIO

(um brol' yoh)

n. Any conflict with an umbrella on a windy day.

URMOMMERIZE
(yer mom' mer eyes)

v. To attempt to decipher *exactly* what an upset coach is mouthing on T.V.

VACUBEAM
(vak' yew beem)

n. The useless headlight on a vacuum cleaner.

VEGEMAT
(vej' mat)

n. The green (or brown) leaf of lettuce that supports a lump of jello or cottage cheese.

WALDUST
(wal' dust)

n. Powder that sticks to you when you lean against a white wooden house.

WASHINGTON, ABRAHAM

(wash' ing tun, ay' bra ham)

n. The unidentifiable President on the facsimile bill on a change machine.

WAVOIDS
(way' voydz)

n. People who bob up and down in the ocean trying to stay dry above the waist.

WESEENEMS
(we see' numz)

n. Recreational vehicles plastered with state national parks and American flag decals.

WHATLET
(hwot' let)

n. Any electrical plate on the wall with no holes, and consequently, no purpose whatsoever.

WOB
(wahb)

n. The long weary walk up the aisle at the end of a movie.

YAFFLING
(yah' fling)

v. Speaking loudly to foreigners as if, somehow, this makes you easier to understand.

YEARAGOSTATS
(yeer' uh goh stats)

n. The part of a forecast that tells you what the weather was like a year ago so you'll feel even more miserable.

YUMP
(yump)

v. To punch one's glove in anticipation of an arriving baseball.

ZEBBITS
(zeb' itz)

n. Those bizarre fireplace tools whose function no one seems able to explain.

ZIPPIJIG
(zih' pih jig)

n. The dance one performs whenever a rubber band is pointed at them.

OFFICIAL SNIGLETS ENTRY BLANK

Dear Rich:

I've searched through every dictionary known to man and cannot find the following word. Why?

____

____

____

____

____

Sincerely,

m(name) ____________________________

(street address) ____________________________

(city, state, zip code) ____________________________

SNIGLETS
P.O. Box 2350
Hollywood, CA 90078